Augustinian Piety and Catholic Reform

Scenes from the Life of Saint Augustine
by the Master of Saint Augustine, active about 1490
Reproduced by permission from The Metropolitan Museum of Art,
The Cloisters Collection, 1961 (61.199)

Augustinian Piety and Catholic Reform

Augustine, Colet, and Erasmus

by

Peter Iver Kaufman

Mercer University Press

ISBN 0-86554-047-0

All books published by Mercer University Press are produced on acid-free paper
which exceeds the minimum standards set by the National Historical
Publications and Records Commission.

Library of Congress Cataloging in Publication Data

Kaufman, Peter Iver.
  Augustinian piety and Catholic reform.

  Includes bibliographical references and index.
  1. Salvation—History of doctrine. 2. Augustine, Saint, Bishop of Hippo—Influence.
3. Erasmus, Desiderius, d. 1536. 4. Colet, John,
1467?-1519. 5. Reformation—Early movements.
I. Title.
BT751.2.K36   1982   234   82-12491
ISBN 0-86554-047-0

Table of Contents

For my family.

Preface

I had originally thought to illustrate the ways in which John Colet and Desiderius Erasmus exploited Augustine's position on the relative roles of grace and human will in the order of salvation. That seems so long ago—though it was not—perhaps because the intention now seems so naive and the project overly ambitious. The complexity of Augustine's legacy prohibits one from speaking with certainty of any single soteriological position that was then (or is presently) clearly more self-evident than rival positions, which might be reconstructed from Augustine's texts. So I started in the sixteenth century, where the book ends, but I have tracked in Augustine's texts and in twelfth-century interpretive material the particular solution to the problem of grace and human will that appealed to Colet and Erasmus. Was it also Augustine's principal solution? I believe so, yet, more important for this study's purposes, I have argued that it was perceived so by Peter Lombard, whom all "accredited" students of theology were obliged to read with care, and by Erasmus in his *Hyperaspistes*, if not before.

Erasmus attributed his rather peculiar brand of synergism to Augustine in the *Hyperaspistes* (1526), but it appeared initially and nearly in full form a quarter of a century earlier in his *Enchiridion*, composed immediately after his return from Colet's Oxford. Colet's influence is apparent. He had formulated his soteriology in his Oxford lectures on the Pauline epistles, against the grain of late medieval scholastic efforts but not necessarily in self-conscious imitation of Augustine or, for that matter, of any other Church Father. By clearing (rather than facing) soteriological problems generated by late medieval scholasticism's various approaches to grace, merit, and personal righteousness, Colet arrived at the voluntarist mysticism characteristic of certain twelfth-century reconceptualizations of Augustine's soteriology. He passed that along to Erasmus and it became characteristic as well of early sixteenth-century Catholic reform.

All this seemed worth discussing and publishing, for it adds a dimension to our understandings of the Augustinian tradition and of the nature of Catholic reform on the eve of the Protestant reformations. Moreover, it suggests the genealogy of Erasmus's soteriology. From one perspective, the study is conservative, perhaps apropos of the alleged conservatism of Catholic reform, for it notes the endurance of a fundamental orientation toward God's presence in personal righteousness. From another, it puts some daring back into *Dogmengeschichte*, which is engaged in a friendly competition for pride of place with studies of popular piety and Reformation demography.

The rather broad interpretation of Augustinian piety, voluntarist mysticism, and Catholic reform that has survived the revisions of aims and intentions omits, in several instances, consideration of technical issues with which I have grappled in journal articles, only parts of which have been blended into chapters one, two, and five. I am grateful to the publishers of *Mediaevalia* (1978), *Augustinian Studies* (1980), and *Augustiniana* (1980) for the opportunity to have discussed the Augustinian soteriological traditions in their pages and again, in modified form, here. Some material for chapter five is adapted with permission from the American Society of Church History from an article that appeared in *Church History* (1977). Several other ideas in the same chapter were first advanced in the pages of *Medievalia et Humanistica* (1981). I owe a substantial debt of gratitude to Mercer University Press for the cooperation that facilitated the manuscript's transformation from ink to print. They have permitted fairly extensive citations in the annotations against which controversial interpretations can be conveniently checked. I wish to thank also the research council of the University of North Carolina at Chapel Hill for a grant that expedited final preparation of the manuscript for publication.

My most profound gratitude is reserved for three instructors and friends. Bernard McGinn challenged my first fumbling efforts to find easy answers to some of the questions raised here. I have profited from his advice but, most often, from his example. To Albert Rabil, Jr. I am indebted for my introduction to Erasmus and for criticisms and suggestions that have made my work more stimulating and more satisfying. Unselfishly he has put his knowledge at my disposal and, at strategic times, he has assured me that they also serve who sit and think. Jerald Brauer supervised my earliest work on Colet and on religion in late medieval and early modern England. From those days to this, he has been a constant source of inspiration and direction. If, at any time, I succeed in dignifying my ideas with the disciplined narration of particulars, this should be credited to him. Among the many other colleagues who have been generous with counsel and encouragement, a special place belongs to Winthrop Hudson. I have counted on conversations with him for insight, valuable criticisms, and an interest in my work that has sustained me when my own enthusiasms sputter. I have been sensible to seek a wide range of suggestions for the improvement of parts or all of this manuscript from the above scholars and from Jill Raitt, Robin Scroggs, and David Steinmetz, who have been too kind to refuse. I have not been as sensible in incorporating all their remarks, and so for what remains implausible, I must shoulder the responsibility.

Bibliographical references have been included in annotations and in close proximity to the first use of traditional abbreviations, making an extensive list unnecessary. Colet's work, however, is relatively unfamiliar, so the reader will wish to take note of the following:*

CONV: *The Sermon of Doctor Colete, Made to the Convocation at Paulis.*

CORP: *De compositione sancti corporis Christi mystici.*

EEC: *Enarratio in Epistolam Primam S. Pauli ad Corinthios.*

EER-a: *Scripta Joannis Colet . . . in Epistolam Divi Pauli ad Romanos.*

EER-b: *Enarratio in Epistolam B. Pauli ad Romanos.*

In Principium Genesios: Scripta Joannis Colet . . . in Principium Genesios.

MARG: *Marginalia* to Marsilius Ficinus, *Epistolae Familiares.*

PSD: *Super opera Dionysii.*

SAC: *Opus de sacramentis ecclesiae.*

*Also see note 55, chapter 2.

Introduction

Popular associations of the word "reformation" with doctrinal reformulation and ecclesiastical restructuring in the sixteenth century until
recently discouraged the rehabilitation of the concept of a Catholic reformation. Other factors as well have conspired, so to speak, to deprive
certain reformers of the sixteenth century's early decades of their rightful
place in the history of that great age of religious controversy. There is the
sense that the Catholic reformers were unsuccessful, as if success could be
equated with the prevention of further protest and Protestant schism.
Catholic reformers, it may be argued, only pointed to abuses or, at best,
proposed only partial remedies. As well-meaning but largely ineffective
moralists they may be assigned the roles of precursors or forerunners or
perhaps branded as apologists. There is also the problem that the last
century's efforts to revive interest in the Catholic reformers in Oxford
and Paris were inspired, to a considerable extent, by national pride and by
the desire to steal from Luther's Saxony or from Burckhardt's Italy some
of the glamour of reformation and renaissance. The results, based upon
selective and often faulty readings of the texts, have been easier to
discredit and jettison than to repair. Finally, and perhaps most damaging,
John Colet and Desiderius Erasmus, principal theorists of Catholic
reform, are understood as eclectic and rather ingenuous students of
theology. Their highly developed sense of God's mysterious presence in,
and claims upon, human experience is frequently overlooked and their

endorsement of the preeminent place of active righteousness in the economy of salvation has been set to one side as but a superficial prolegomenon to the complicated soteriologies of more outspoken reformers. The upshot is that Catholic reform has been judged as "mere moralism" and as a more or less insignificant moment in the history of the Christian traditions. But without denying that the Catholic reformation of Colet and Erasmus concentrated with remarkable insistence on the development of a doctrine of Christian life, to which other doctrinal reformulations and institutional policies were discernibly subordinated, the scholar may still detect a substratum of conviction that connects the Catholic Reformation with several themes in the multiplex Augustinian tradition of medieval Christianity.

I believe that to make this connection is to achieve a more profoundly historical appreciation of sixteenth-century Catholic reform. Although rewarding, this is also risky business. On the one hand, Colet and Erasmus were relatively unconcerned at first with the pedigree of their notions of personal righteousness and church reform. They were instead preoccupied with the application of practical or moral reasoning to the instruction in the Pauline epistles, to the lessons of personal experience, and to the predicament of the late medieval church. On the other hand, there simply is no uncontested interpretation of Augustine or of the rich soteriological tradition that evolved from his work. The present study risks excessive valuation of a single theme in Augustine's theology, divine and human collaboration in personal righteousness. This is not intended to revise contemporary comprehension of Augustine's objectives but, more modestly, to restore the picture of Augustine that evidently appealed to the Catholic reformers and to suggest that this restoration has some foundation in the texts. To do more, that is, to enter more responsibly into the conversation about Augustine's own enterprise, would demand much greater attention to competing assessments than that presently given them in the first chapter.

Likewise, the second chapter, "An Augustinian Tradition in the Twelfth Century," is less ambitious than it may initially appear. Augustine's sense of God's mysterious collaboration with human will seems to have predisposed Peter Lombard to accept that God's unmediated presence in human will ennobled personal righteousness. Alongside Peter's presentation of Augustine's anti-Pelagian polemic, which has been taken to reduce radically the soteriological importance of human volition and to exclude from the *ordo salutis* moral theology, this voluntarist mysticism surfaced as a way of speaking of the coefficiency of divine and human wills. The trail of voluntarist mysticism is not easily found and followed in the twelfth century or in the labyrinthian logic of late medieval nominalisms. Exploration certainly could not be considered complete until Anselm and Bernard in the twelfth century and, inter alia, Bradwardine, Gerson, and Biel in the later medieval periods have been much more exhaustively questioned than they have been here. My concern is to call attention to the presence of voluntarist mysticism in the twelfth century, to note the possibility of its persistence as later theologians wrestled with the authority of Augustine and with the problem of grace and human will, but especially to demonstrate the priority of this theme, that is, the significance of unmediated divine and human collaboration, for Colet, Erasmus, and their Catholic reformation.

Colet may seem to be out of his element. I believe, however, that his Oxford lectures forge an important link between certain concepts of righteousness in the Augustinian tradition and the concept of righteousness highly influential in Catholic reform. Colet's long but not unusually protracted progress toward the degree of Doctor of Divinity (1483-1504) was presumably channeled through the customary reading of Augustine and Peter Lombard. He elected to forgo lectures on Peter's *Sentences* and to devote his university lectures to St. Paul's letters. His purpose, it seems, was to recapture initiative from scholastics who dominated religious reflection and to return to an authentically Pauline doctrine of the Christian life. Something of a medieval scholastic *manqué*, Colet (and then Erasmus) presented a lean version of scholastic soteriologies, one that restored mystery to moral theology.

What began years ago as a study of Colet's soteriology, the silhouette of which is still discernible in this volume, has become a study of the meaning of personal righteousness in the Catholic reform and of the importance for Colet and Erasmus of voluntarist mysticism, which permits us to think of Catholic reform as an Augustinian tradition early in the sixteenth century.

1   *Augustine's Pursuit of Righteousness and the Question of Church Reform*

The Problem of Conversion in a Century of Change

Less than a century before Augustine's conversion to Christianity and subsequent ordination in 391, Constantine, as one of several contestants for Roman *imperium*, was attracted to Christianity. As he eliminated his political opposition, first in the western and later in the eastern portions of the empire, Christians who trembled with fear during the persecutions of his predecessors, Diocletian and Galerius, grew confident that some divinely intended deliverance was at hand. Many attributed Constantine's military and political successes to his conversion and, as a matter of course, ascribed his conversion to God's benevolence toward his long-suffering church. But the young and gifted emperor was interested more in the pragmatic consequences than in the theological significance of his conversion, and he set to work organizing ecclesiastical institutions and assisting in the definition of doctrines as if Christian institutions and ideas were weights and measures that might bring cohesion, if not uniformity, to the Mediterranean world. The sudden shift in one man's loyalties started a series of changes that transformed the estate of religion in the Roman world, not once but several times before the close of the fourth century. The acceptance of Christianity as a religion of state, the alternating triumphs of Athanasian and Arian Christianity, and the shortlived revival of official paganism left few Christian ideas and attitudes unchanged. It could be said that the events of the fourth century dramatized the need for a greater understanding of change in the now "authorized" church, which had been subjected to so much of it. More specifically, Christian theology had not yet scrupulously examined the momentous changes of personal allegiances and political orders with the intent of articulating the complex relationship between divine initiative in such changes and human responsibility for them. Had Augustine not undergone his own profound conversion as the eventful century drew to a close, his attempts to state the problem and find a solution might not have been as persistent as they were; but one senses that not much more time could have elapsed before the question of divine initiative and human volition in redemptive transformations became the steady diet of Christian theologians.

The conversion of an entire empire and the regeneration of the recalcitrant sinner, despite obvious dissimilarities, may be seen as parallel cases of divine reclamation. In the one, the church is vindicated and history is won for God and for God's elect; in the other, the soul is rescued from and fortified against worldly temptations. The conversion of the Roman empire must have appeared to have been an unmistakable sign of divine benevolence and power. An able apologist would have incorporated so splendid an episode in his vindication of God's guidance of historical affairs, and it is surprising that Augustine entered very little about Constantine in his monumental *De civitate Dei*.[1] The conversion of the sinner, the second level of reclamation, was of special significance to the theologian who kept the care of souls uppermost in his mind. Augustine elected to engage the issue of the relationship between divine and human causalities in redemptive activity at this level, where divine initiative must be explained in terms of personal encounters between the derelict, the stubborn, and the penitent and their God. Whether he wrote

---

[1]Augustine, *De civitate Dei* 5.25. But as Augustine made his way through the reigns of Constantine and Theodosius, he maintained that the successes of Rome served the purposes of God. Nevertheless, Augustine was mindful that, after having received Christ's promises, no Christian ought to expect another earthly Jerusalem. This may well account for his reluctance to specify the place assigned to Constantine by divine providence. See Giuseppe Amari, *Il concetto di storia in S. Agostino* (Rome, 1951); Jules Chaix-Ruy, "La Cité de Dieu et la structure du temps chez Saint Augustin," *Augustinus Magister* 2 (Paris, 1954):923-31; and L. G. Patterson, *God and History in Early Christian Thought* (New York, 1967), pp. 103-31.

for the correction or for the condemnation of the heterodox, on the harmony of the gospels or on the utility of fasting, he was mindful of the problems involved in charting the Christian's passage from sin to liberty and he sought to instruct his readers about the proportional significances of grace and human will, especially after Pelagius appeared to have upset the balance.

Continuity in Augustine's Position on Righteousness

The good instructor skillfully employs his experience to illustrate and, in part, to verify the lesson. Augustine went one step further: in his *Confessions* and apparently in much of his polemical writing, his personal experience was the lesson. He had intimate knowledge that God's providential hand worked in conversion and he testified that the Christian's recognition of God's unseen prodding and sustaining influence would guarantee that the wholesome reorientation achieved in conversion would be a lasting one.

The test of endurance was the closest Augustine came to furnishing a touchstone with which others might confirm the authenticity of their own conversions. Faith in the divine management of personal transformations was the foundation for endurance but such faith was difficult to obtain. It was more likely that a person might be rescued from the thick undergrowth of frivolous habits and practices that retarded progress toward true wisdom and happiness and yet attribute the rescue to circumstance or to the kindness of friends and advisors. If Augustine were correct, the inadequacy of the response would soon tell in the impermanence of the result. By way of illustration, Augustine recounted the experience of his friend Alypius. This particular young man chanced to hear Augustine, then a Manichaean schoolmaster, clarify a passage with an anecdote that awakened him to his own immoderation and converted him to continence. Neither Augustine nor Alypius, who would later be truly converted and become, like Augustine, a Christian bishop, guessed at the time that God had ordained the crucial classroom event; therefore, neither man called upon God to sustain the conversion. Alypius was soon back to his old ways,[2] yet the lesson of Alypius's precipitous relapse

---

[2] *Conf.* 6.7.11-8.13.

became the very heart of Augustine's *Confessions*, namely, that without a firm faith (*"fides solida"*) in God's providential guidance there could be no perseverance in righteousness, no complete regeneration, hence no meaningful conversion.[3]

Augustine filled the *Confessions* with his memories of youthful indiscretions and intellectual temerity, and with his recollections of the significant turning points in his career, but speculations that might have elucidated his "firm faith" in divine initiative were not deliberately and systematically set forth. Probably for this reason some persons read Augustine's report of his persistent personal struggles as justification for their own high estimation of human will. To Augustine, however, his time of restlessness and vain searching was ground for self-reproach. If his adolescent defiance, his carnal and intellectual promiscuity, and his wrongheaded infatuation with Manichaean doctrine proved anything, they demonstrated the patience, benevolence, and power of God and not the vigor of human will. The fact that Augustine emerged triumphant, that is, converted to his true religion, had relatively little to do with the tenacity of his will. In Augustine's opinion, his eventual conversion attested to the patient, benevolent, and forceful exercise of divine initiative.[4] His confidence in divine patience was a corollary to his trust in divine predestination. God foreknew that Augustine would undergo a profound transformation—and for the consolation of his pious mother, revealed as much to her in a dream—and kept a vigil over lesser changes and over Augustine's inconstant and infelicitous behavior until the time was appropriate for his momentous conversion.[5] God's willingness to redeem the most desperate souls, among whom Augustine numbered himself, testified to divine benevolence as did the parables of the prodigal son and the lost sheep.[6] Finally, the powerful thrust of divine initiative was manifest in the conversion of truly wicked souls. Rather than enroll

---

[3] Ibid. 6.11.20.

[4] See Karl Holl, "Augustins innere Entwicklung," *Gesammelte Aufsätze zur Kirchengeschichte* 3 (Tübingen, 1928): 67: "Versteht es sich, dass Augustin selbst den übermächtigen Antrieb in seinem Innern als eine Wirkung Gottes verstand, der ihm in jeder Stunde sein *evigila, evigila* zugerufen hatte."

[5] *Conf.* 3.11.19-20.

[6] Ibid. 8.3.6.

himself in this class, however, Augustine used the story of the conversion of Victorinus, an orator notorious for bedeviling Christians, to preface his tale of the significant moments in his own conversion. It was as if Augustine were assuring himself that the God whose power was sufficient to turn the talents of a bitter antagonist to the service of the true religion was certainly able to redeem his own reckless yet sincerely inquiring mind.[7] In the eighth book of the *Confessions* Augustine brought the narrative of his personal struggles to some resolution. The earlier books documented the yearnings of an earnest, if not always courageous will; but they contributed to the meaning of the autobiography only inasmuch as they prepared for the testimony of Augustine's conversion, testimony that all thanks for Augustine's reorientation were due to the benevolent and effective assistance of God.

At one end of conversion, we hear of Augustine's agonized indecision ("I saw myself and was horrified by what I saw, yet there was no place to flee from myself");[8] at the other end we encounter the believer's genuine dedication. Somehow the enfeebled will has been empowered and the distracted will has been quickened: it has become possible for the believer to will by all means and "with his whole will."[9] The reader of Augustine's *Confessions* will be conscious of passing from one condition to the other, and yet he will sense that he has passed through a dark tunnel and has little understanding of what transpired en route. Augustine's affirmation of divine initiative appears axiomatic, as does his profound sense of dependence upon divine benevolence and power;[10] nevertheless, the outcome of conversion, to some extent, suggests an "independent" act of the will, for how can one speak of genuine dedication if that disposition is forged under duress or under some more subtle kind of compulsion? Indeed, Augustine told of his own uneven progress from impiety to an

---

[7]Ibid. 8.4.9: "Quanto igitur gratius cogitabatur Victorini pectus, quod tanquam inexpugnabile receptaculum diabolus obtinuerat, et Victorini lingua, quo telo grandi et acuto multos peremerat; tanto abundantius exsultare oportuit filios tuos, quia Rex noster alligavit fortem, et videbant vasa ejus erepta mundari, et aptari in honorem tuum, et fieri utilia Domino ad omne opus bonum."

[8]Ibid. 8.7.16.

[9]Ibid. 8.8.20, 10.24.

[10]Ibid. 10.40.65.

acknowledgment of his iniquity and finally to a desire to stand steadfastly in divine favor—all of which is symptomatic of the efforts of an essentially righteous, though perhaps timid, will.[11] Although these efforts, at Augustine's insistence, must not be calculated as the cause for divine assistance and for conversion, a nagging question remains: to what extent does human effort figure in conversion, in righteousness, and in redemption?

Augustine was not permitted to develop a definitive answer to this complex question in peace. Some readers impolitely jumped to their own conclusions and pressed the presiding genius of Mediterranean Christianity to work out the lessons of his conversion experience in the context of theological controversy. Chief among those who successively embarrassed, annoyed, and infuriated Augustine was Pelagius, who had captivated Roman audiences with his contention that humankind possessed the ability to achieve the good that God intended when he had created human nature.[12] One of Pelagius's more outspoken disciples, Coelestius, crossed to Carthage in 411 and challenged Augustine's understandings of sin and grace with extravagant assertions for which the African Bishop later blamed Pelagius himself. Coelestius alleged that the good of creation was recapitulated by every birth, that it was possible for and incumbent upon each person to be as sinless as Adam before the Fall, and therefore that God's grace assists man only by demonstrating with example and doctrine what man must do. Augustine immediately responded from the pulpit and with a treatise on infant baptism.[13] He registered the objection

---

[11]Ibid. 8.1.1.

[12]On Pelagius, see G. de Plinval, *Pélage, ses écrits, sa vie et sa réforme* (Lausanne, 1943); Torgny Bohlin, *Die Theologie des Pelagius und ihre Genesis* (Uppsala, 1957); and de Plinval's response to Bohlin, "Points de vues récents sur la théologie de Pélage," *Recherches de science réligieuse* 40 (1958):228-32. Also consult Robert F. Evans, *Pelagius: Inquiries and Reappraisals* (New York, 1968); and Adolar Zumkeller, "Neuinterpretation oder Verzeichnung der Gnadenlehre des Pelagius und seines Gegners Augustinus?" *Augustinian Studies* 5 (1974): 209-26.

[13]*Sermo* 294.16.16-19.18; and *De peccatorum meritis et remissione* 2.6.7. The controversy centered on Augustine's appreciation of the indispensability of infant baptism, an appreciation resting on the witness of scripture and church tradition as well as on the pastoral context of the sacrament itself. See *De pecc. mer.* 1.34.64; and Vittorino Grossi, "Il battesimo e la polemica pelagiani negli anni 411/413," *Augustinianum* 9 (1969): 45-54.

that the condition of Adam after the Fall endured as the condition of every individual.[14] Augustine was persuaded that the constant ministration of grace was required not only to demonstrate what man must do but also to restore to human will the possibility of doing what must be done.

Although persons had been created with a good will, Augustine was unconvinced that the sustained performance of good was possible without divine assistance. This was true for Adam before the Fall and much more so for the heirs of his indiscretion. Adam, according to Augustine, was created with the ability to avoid sin (and therefore death) but not with an enduring inability to sin. To put this in a slightly different way, one would say that as long as the rattles of sadness and fear had not sounded and insofar as human instincts and faculties submitted spontaneously to reason and will, Adam was a free agent but not a necessarily moral agent. The modest influence of grace was necessary to assure perseverance in righteousness and hence to protect primordial freedom. What remained of free choice in fallen man required all the more assistance. Grace was then necessary not only to assure perseverance in righteousness but to silence despair and fear and to acquire the possibility for righteousness lost by Adam for all his descendants.[15]

What actually happened to Adam and by what means the unfortunate modification was transmitted to his heirs concerned Augustine less than the effects of Adam's Fall upon the order of each person's faculties. Augustine argued that as a result of the very first sin of disobedience, flesh contends against the spirit, the passions rebel against reason and will, and carnal concupiscence and unrelenting social conflicts surface as discernible symptoms of the forfeiture of the soul's life in free and spontaneous submission to God. Very soon after his conversion, in one of his discussions of Genesis, Augustine observed that reason and will were yoked to

---

[14]*De pecc. mer.* 1.26.39; 1.32.61; 2.7.8; and 3.13.22. Augustine suggested that Coelestius had not dared to attack directly the practice of infant baptism "ne tam firmata salubriter Ecclesiae consuetudo violatores suos ferre non possit" (3.13.22). But the Bishop considered that the assailant's repudiation of original sin undermined the need for sacramental remission with respect to the newborn.

[15]See A. Solignac, "La Condition de l'homme pechéur d'après S. Augustin," *Nouveau revue théologique* 78 (1956): 361.

the body's base desires and completely dominated by them.[16] The disequilibrium that derived from a single yet telling transgression issued in a perversion of human powers that robbed the good will of its effectiveness and held free choice captive. Later, when he wrote his *Confessions*, Augustine found that his preconversion hesitancy and indecision validated precisely this observation.

Augustine's controversies with the Pelagians orbited around the issue of human will's captivity. The question whether Pelagius believed that there was in man an innate power to overcome evil or that only the baptized Christian had sufficient power to pursue righteousness is still debated, but there is no disagreement about the proposition that Pelagians were vastly more confident than Augustine in the Christian's command over his own conduct. If that command were denied and the extent of the will's captivity overstated, Pelagians were fearful that the essentially Manichaean doctrine of the inevitability of evil would be corroborated.[17] According to Augustine, they preferred to think of evil as the works of the flesh and the habits that those works built up and reinforced but not as the flesh itself.[18] Birth did not impose evil upon the individual and no original sin was passed down through generations to confound humankind's best impulses. On the contrary, inasmuch as each birth reenacted the good of God's creation, human nature is endowed with the ability to break the hold of habit and (with the aid of law and perhaps with grace communicated in baptism) to liberate will from its bondage to sin.[19] In short, the Christian possessed freedom *from* captivity.

Augustine's understanding of evil was predicated upon a doctrine of original sin and an acceptance of its mysterious transmission to all humankind. It was impossible, given Augustine's understanding, for man to possess as a birthright the freedom and ability to break the bonds of sin

---

[16]*De Genesi contra Manichaeos* 2.11.15. Also see Evodius Braem, "Augustinus' leer over de heiligmakende genada," *Augustiniana* 3 (1953): 329-30; and Henri Rondet, "La Théologie de saint Augustin prédicateur," *Bulletin de littérature ecclésiastique* 72 (1971): 99-100.

[17]In what follows, however, our concern is with Augustine's perception of Pelagius's and Pelagian positions and not, for the most part, with the positions themselves.

[18]*De natura et gratia* 64.76.

[19]See Evans, *Pelagius: Inquiries and Reappraisals*, pp. 96-102.

(freedom *from* captivity), yet it was not impossible for man to retain some vestige of primordial freedom *in* captivity. To meet the challenge of what he perceived as Pelagius's naturalism, Augustine poured enormous energy into his carefully considered, but not always consistent, evaluations of free choice in fallen man. Faced with two basically undesirable alternatives—either posit evil's inevitability or assume man's ability to liberate his own will— Augustine elected instead to ask what free choice signified at the level at which one was no longer "free for righteousness" but appeared to be free only to court danger in a world where "the good" was likely to be identified with whatever might momentarily gratify the ruling instincts.[20] He answered that free choice was simply the freedom to do good or evil, but that in captivity the choice to do good was not complemented by the power to accomplish the chosen good.[21] The tragedy of fallen humanity then was not that anyone was programmed to follow a particular predetermined course without fail but rather that the loss of the pristine order of human faculties removed the one possibility that gave meaning to human freedom. Augustine was speaking of the power to will by all means and thereby to achieve the desired good. Beneath Augustine's understanding of captive free choice lay the conviction that the best that fallen humanity could do alone was not good enough to recover the primitive order and liberty fumbled away by his ill-fated ancestor.

Having exposed the inferiority of free choice in fallen humanity to the primordial liberty of Adam, Augustine could not simply deny soteriological significance to the inferior variety of freedom and abandon man to hopelessness. At its best, free choice in fallen humanity could lead to melancholy and perhaps to an appeal for assistance to make an end of the sinner's misfortunes. This was the hallmark of that inalienable freedom (*"liberum arbitrium congenitum et omnino inamissibile"*), which, paraphrasing Augustine, keeps alive the desire for blessed liberty in those who may also be driven by contrary desires.[22]

---

[20]*Contra duas epistolas Pelagianorum* 2.5.9-10.

[21]*De gratia et libero arbitrio* 4.7.

[22]*Contra secundam Juliani responsionem opus imperfectum* 6.11: "Nam si, ut dicis, boni malique voluntarii possibilitas sola libertas est; non habet libertatem Deus, in quo

Augustine resisted the pessimism toward which his assertions of the will's captivity inclined, even as he resented what appeared to him as the undue optimism of the Pelagians. It could be said that, to an appreciable extent, Augustine and Pelagius were in league against a common enemy, Manichaeanism. They agreed that some latent promise of redemption existed in the disorder of the human condition despite the captivity of the will.[23] Both were reluctant to consign creation once and for all to the evil powers present and pervasive therein, and yet they disagreed as to humankind's ability to retrieve and to restore the good of creation. Pelagians argued that scripture would not have demanded the impossible and that, insofar as scripture imposed certain moral obligations upon the Christian, one should reasonably infer that the Christian could accomplish what was demanded of him without the intervention of extraordinary powers. Augustine quickly caught the scent of a *non sequitur* here: the enormous power that, according to Augustine, Pelagians attributed to free choice could not rest on a flimsy foundation that, in essence, wrongly deduced human ability from religious obligation.[24] St. Paul's experience of the tension between the good that one wills and ought to will and the evil that one actually does (Romans 7:19-25) documented exactly the opposite of what, as Augustine understood their argument, the Pelagians hoped to prove biblically.[25] Augustine's experience confirmed his suspicion that the twin notions that a person ought to and can achieve righteousness did not preclude prevenient and persistent divine assistance but actually made such assistance necessary. He contended that the Pelagian argument, when contemplated along with a sober assessment of

---

peccandi possibilitas non est. Hominis vero liberum arbitrium congenitum et omnino inamissibile si quaerimus, illud est quo beati omnes esse volunt, etiam hi qui ea nolunt quae ad beatitudinem ducunt."

[23]See Bohlin, *Die Theologie des Pelagius*, p. 104; and John Morris, "Pelagian Literature," *The Journal of Theological Studies* 16 (1965): 55.

[24]*De perfectione justitiae hominis* 3.5: "Cum enim videmus claudum, qui sanari potest, recte utique dicimus, Debet homo iste esse sine claudicatione; et si debet, potest. Nec tamen cum vult, continuo potest; sed cum fuerit adhibita curatione sanatus, et medicina adjuverit voluntatem. Hoc fit in interiore homine, quod ad peccatum attinet tanquam ejus claudicationem, per ejus gratiam qui venit non vocare justos, sed peccatores; quia non est opus sanis medicus, sed male habentibus."

[25]Note the earlier use made of this passage in Augustine's *Confessiones* 7.21.27.

the captivity of the will, posed a dilemma from which only grace could grant relief. Prevenient grace assisted the will, first to desire righteousness and then to consent freely to further divine aid that would make possible the achievement of righteousness. Long before the outbreak of his controversies with the Pelagians, Augustine wrote his reflections *De diversis quaestionibus ad Simplicianum* in which he predicated deliverance from captivity on the operation of a prevenient grace. Familiarity with Pelagian propositions led him to refine that judgment.[26]

Quite consistent with his position in the *De diversis quaestionibus*, Augustine's later charges against the Pelagians amounted to an injunction to take seriously Philippians 2:13 ("God is at work in you, both to will and to work for his good pleasure") and not to overestimate the preceding mandate to work out one's own salvation (2:12).[27] Augustine was most distressed by what he perceived as Pelagius's more or less consistent naturalism, which conceived of righteousness under the aegis of morality. He countered by enjoining his adversaries to think theologically about righteousness, which, he preached, demanded that we find in God's work in us the sole source of hope that we can work out our own salvation.[28] But, according to Augustine, Pelagius sadly underestimated the human will's disability and was therefore disinclined to heed his injunction. Whatever else Augustine thought of Pelagian efforts to minimize the extent of the will's captivity, he found inexcusable the Pelagian blindness to the necessity of God's constant work in us, not simply in the creation of human will but in its preparation for divine assistance and in the actual assistance that enabled the will to pursue righteousness.[29] When the

---

[26]*Ad Simplicianum de diversis quaestionibus* 1.2.12. The replies to Simplicianus reveal Augustine's increasingly acute consciousness of the universality of sin (e.g., 1.2.17) as well as his growing appreciation for the importance of divine initiative in the *initium salutis*. Note Alberto Pincherle, *La formazione teologica di S. Agostino* (Rome, n.d.) 162-63.

[27]*De spiritu et littera* 29.50; *De nat. et gr.* 27.31; *De gr. et lib. arb.* 9.21.

[28]See, inter alia, *Ser.* 153.7.8; 168.5.5; 265.9.10; 297.4.5-5.7. Also review Fidelis Schnitzler, *Zur Theologie der Verkündigung in den Predigten des hl. Augustinus* (Freiburg, 1968), pp. 113-34, for a discussion of Augustine's view of the work of God in the very act of preaching.

[29]See *Enchiridion ad Laurentium* 32 for one of the most succinct and nimble expressions of his argument.

knowledgment of such a necessity was seen to have the
re, as Augustine documented to his satisfaction in his
..ien the course of life admitted of divine interventions,
ranged from the subtle and covert to the truly miraculous, as
Augustine contended in his *Confessions*; and when personal and political
history had been reviewed as the restoration of a sinful soul or of an
estranged people to God, the Bishop's favorite theme, then it was nigh
impossible for Augustine to contemplate the will and its exercise as
purely natural phenomena. Clearly he was horrified that Pelagius and his
disciples appeared to have done just that.[30]

One might guess from what has been said thus far that the line of
demarcation between Augustine and the Pelagians allowed no trespass.
To the extent that from 396 the confidence in divine patience, benevolence, and power that Augustine voiced in his *Confessions* increased and
influenced all that he wrote and to the extent that the opinions about
grace and human will posited in the *De diversis quaestionibus* steadily
found their way into his later anti-Pelagian treatises, one's guess would be
essentially correct—especially if one keeps in mind the important fact
that the dividing line was of Augustine's invention, that he scrupulously
remained on the one side and consistently placed Pelagius on the other.
Nevertheless, it should be asked whether the position that Augustine
held before 396 and after his conversion and subsequent ordination in 391
was similar to the position that he assumed in his *Confessions* and against
the Pelagians. In other words, if we extend Augustine's line of demarcation backward from 396, will we still find him on the side that he later
stalwartly defended? The question is all the more pressing because
Pelagius cited Augustine's early essay on the origin of evil, the *De libero
arbitrio voluntatis*, which was written between 389 and 395, in support of

---

[30]*De nat. et gr.* 53.62. Note Alfred Vanneste's consideration of the question of human
nature's "autosuffisance" in the *De natura et gratia* ("Nature et grâce dans la théologie de
saint Augustin," *Recherches Augustiniennes* 10[1975]: 161-62). Vanneste explained that
the force of Pelagian arguments probably required Augustine to forgo any thought of
synthesis and to stress the theme of *natura vitiata* so persistently. "On peut néanmoins
regretter, d'un point de vue abstrait et idéal, que, pour réfuter Pélage, il se soit trop
souvent contenté d'invoquer quelques textes bibliques plus ou moins isolés, sans essayer
de comparer, au niveau le plus profond, la théologie biblique da la grâce et la philosophie
grecque et stoicienne de la nature" (p. 166).

certain propositions that Augustine resolutely placed on the side opposite his own. In order to respond more precisely, I have transformed the question into two related inquiries, and I have asked first whether Augustine's early comments on man's responsibility for evil contradict his later views and, secondly, whether Augustine's later understanding of the will's captivity departed from his understanding of the same problem in the *De libero arbitrio voluntatis.*

The intention of Augustine's earliest treatise on free choice was not to explore the range of the will's operation (with or without divine assistance). The treatise was rather a rebuttal to the Manichaean argument that the God who created all things was responsible for the existence of evil. The allegedly absurd alternatives, as the Manichaeans outlined them, were either to deny God's sovereignty or to plead that evil was "no thing." In either case, the effort to exonerate God would lead to enormous theological and terminological difficulties. Augustine, however, was not prepared to gainsay divine sovereignty, to blame God for the existence of evil, or to concede the unreality of evil. Another strategy was possible: one could speak of evil as privation, as that which "exists" as deficiency. God did not create the deficiency, but, according to Augustine, God endowed humankind with a certain growth potential and with free choice that might frustrate and inhibit growth and thereby occasion deficiency.[31] Divine generosity, therefore, was not at fault when man freely betrayed his calling; each man must bear the responsibility for his own betrayal and for the imperfections and privations that follow as consequences. The first question then appears to find an easy answer. While laboring to solve the Manichaean conundrum, at one point, Augustine hinted that Adam's fall had not made evil an inevitable and virtually inescapable part of the human condition. Evil, after all, might be "natural" as well as penal. (His doctrine of original sin and his solemn appreciation of Adam's pervasive impact upon humankind developed more fully in later expositions of Genesis.) Therefore, insofar as Augustine held each person responsible for his own sinfulness, Pelagius could justifiably cite his adversary's early treatise in order to substantiate his own views on the question of evil.

---

[31]*De libero arbitrio voluntatis* 3.22.65.

Surprisingly, a correct answer to the first question can result in a misleading response to the second. If it can be said that Augustine credited man with the will and power to pursue righteousness, then one might coast to the conclusion that Augustine's more severe depiction of the will's captivity and consequent reliance for its rescue upon prevenient grace represented a marked departure from his position in 395. This conclusion, in turn, would undermine the supposition that Augustine's reflections on the collaboration of grace and will were founded upon his conversion experience. Furthermore, this conclusion places Augustine in the uncomfortable position of turning back upon himself in the anti-Pelagian treatises and sinking his teeth in his own tail. Alternatively, one might take Augustine at his word: in his later essays he was not withdrawing an earlier expressed confidence in human will but rather declaiming against wrongheaded Pelagian distillations of the *De libero arbitrio voluntatis*.[32] Augustine could quite legitimately claim that his early commentary had not assumed that man was autonomous in either choosing the good or effectively pursuing righteousness. Only with the help of its creator could the soul acquire virtue and break the bondage of the will.[33] Presupposing that help, Augustine spoke optimistically of the possibility that human will might overcome evil. This is not to say, in response to the second question, that Augustine's understanding of divine assistance underwent no change and recurred evenly or uniformly in his diverse treatises. I have argued here for continuity but not for seamless consistency. The proper response acknowledges that Augustine's thoughts about the nature of the will's bondage and the role of grace in the will's liberation developed as the need for greater precision in his

----

[32]*Retractationes* 1.9.4: "Quod in aliis opusculis nostris satis egimus, istos inimicos hujus gratiae novos haereticos refellentes; quamvis et in his libris, qui non contra illos omnino, quippe illi nondum erant, sed contra Manichaeos conscripti sunt, de Libero Arbitrio; non omnimodo de ista Dei gratia reticuimus, quam nefanda impietate conantur auferre."

[33]*De lib. arb. vol.* 2.20.54; and 3.20.57. Also see M. Huftier, "Libre arbitre, liberté et péché chez saint Augustin," *Recherches de théologie ancienne et médiévale* 33 (1966): 190-91. As he was completing the *De libero arbitrio voluntatis*, Augustine was developing the same ideas in his expositions of Romans and Galatians (394). See Max Wundt, "Ein Wendepunkt in Augustins Entwicklung," *Zeitschrift für die neutestamentliche Wissenschaft und die Kunde der älteren Kirche* 21 (1922): 54-55.

general reliance upon grace became more urgent, yet there was no cause for recantation on the issue of human will's dependence upon the inspiration and sustaining influence of grace.

De Gratia et Libero Arbitrio

At times during the extended Pelagian controversy Augustine championed grace so eagerly and energetically that his defense of divine initiative appeared to overstate the enduring reality of sin and the tragedy of human helplessness. Yet whereas Augustine's anti-Pelagian treatises lost the more optimistic point of view of the *De libero arbitrio voluntatis*, they confirmed the position, for the most part implicit in the earlier essay, that human will required constant divine assistance. This confirmation became the chief strategy in Augustine's counteroffensive against Pelagius and his followers. For my purposes, it is important to note that the later argument elaborated on the earliest expression of Augustine's confirmation in two meaningful ways. First, from the *De libero arbitrio*'s definition of Christian liberty as submission to truth,[34] Augustine inferred that free choice in fallen man could be neither truly nor supremely free. What remained to be done and what the Bishop did in fact do, largely in response to Pelagian misreadings of his early essay, was to devise a system that would distinguish between degrees of freedom. Adam's choice was less circumscribed than the allegedly free choices of his heirs, who must be liberated by grace in order to will by all means their own submission to God and salvation. Second, Augustine continued to explore the possibility that divine predestination and human freedom were actually compatible, a possibility he raised and argued before his astonished interlocuter in the *De libero arbitrio voluntatis*.[35] In his anti-Manichaean theodicy, he was interested in the compatibility of predestination with humanity's freedom to sin (and responsibility for sin). But as his preliminary explorations of the possible coexistence of foreknowledge and authentic human choice developed in the context of his soteriology, he shaped his understanding of divine and human collab-

---

[34]*De lib. arb. vol.* 2.13.37.

[35]Ibid. 3.3.8. Augustine did not think to oppose freedom to predestination until 429 (cf. *De praedestinatione sanctorum*).

oration in works of righteousness. Augustine's final position surfaced in his treatise *De gratia et libero arbitrio*, a document that continued his battle against Pelagius and yet wrestled with extremists who, also reacting against Pelagian claims, so bleached human will of its power that subsequent assertions of divine sovereignty threatened to subvert human participation in the *ordo salutis* and promote complacency.

As a result of his confrontation with the Pelagians, Augustine was probably alert to the possibility that readers could be led astray by some of his remarks. Nevertheless, he may have been mildly shocked when he learned that certain monks in the prosperous North African town of Hadrumentum supposed that they followed Augustine when they greatly minimized the redemptive importance of free choice in fallen man. At the very beginning of his treatise *De gratia et libero arbitrio* Augustine fraternally addressed those who had been carried to this intolerably and untenably extreme position by the vehemence of their own defense of divine initiative.[36] While wary of Pelagians who would be likely to scan each of his new treatises, eager to catch their old and most articulate adversary in a contradiction, Augustine was now concerned to correct those for whom his own affirmation of grace corresponded to a denial of freedom. That this should have been Augustine's predicament raises doubts about the clarity and precision of his earlier remarks against heterodoxy; however, in his defense, one might cite the stubborn tendency in Christian thought to view justification and sanctification *either* as self-determined *or* as divinely determined affairs despite many skillful attempts at compromise. Augustine's *De gratia et libero arbitrio* was and is a direct challenge to that tendency, to which Augustine presumably never intended to contribute.

To be sure, Augustine's compromise was unwavering on what he believed to be essential to Christian soteriology. His contention that we can will nothing advantageously without God's assistance remained unaltered in the *De gratia et libero arbitrio* and was, if anything, more persistently reemphasized. Divine initiative was necessary to prepare human will (*"De operante illo ut velimus"*) and to enable man to cooper-

---

[36]*De gr. et lib. arb.* 1.1.

ate with God in pious works.[37] For some, the preliminary initiative may take the form of fear, to others God may first contribute confidence.[38] According to Augustine, one cannot discern and certainly not dictate the manner in which God elects to incline human will, but one ought not doubt that God acts righteously even when certain wills are left to languish in sin.

Augustine's proclamation of divine initiative did not discourage Etienne Gilson from speculating that the Bishop foresaw that human will must deliberately consent to receive preliminary divine prompting.[39] But unless "consent" is broadly conceived, Gilson's fascinating observation is ultimately unacceptable. The fact that free choice remains in the fallen did not signify for Augustine that human will piously "acts" in receiving God's first subtle gestures. We can infer from Augustine's survey of his own conversion in the *Confessions* that he would not have contended that one was immediately conscious of the very first influences of divine initiative. Only as human will grows in grace does the Christian acknowledge what Augustine advocated in his *Confessions* and again in the *De gratia et libero arbitrio*, namely, the idea that God crowns with perfection that which grace, and not will, initiated.[40] This does not mean, however, that Augustine narrowly considered human will as the material cause of God's salvific action. Human will was not stamped with righteous intentions nor coerced to pursue the good but "inclined." Divine initiative should be thought of as an invitation extended to human will, an invitation to will by all means and therefore to acquire the power to accomplish

---

[37]Ibid. 7.17. Also consult R. P. Deman, "La Théologie de la grâce," *Augustinus Magister* 3 (Paris, 1954): 247-50; Gotthard Nygren, *Das Prädestinationsproblem in der Theologie Augustins* (Göttingen, 1956), pp. 69-102; and Athanase Sage, "Praeparatur voluntas a Domino," *Revue des études augustiniennes* 10 (1964): 1-20.

[38]*De gr. et lib. arb.* 9.21. Also note *Ad Simpl.* 1.2.13: "posset ita vocare, quomodo illis aptum esset, ut et moverentur."

[39]Etienne Gilson, *The Christian Philosophy of Saint Augustine*, trans. L. E. M. Lynch (New York, 1967), pp. 161-62. Also see John M. Rist, "Augustine on Free Will and Predestination," *The Journal of Theological Studies* 20 (1969): 434-39 for a different and suggestive analysis of Gilson's contention with respect to the presumed irresistibility of grace.

[40]*De gr. et lib. arb.* 6.15; 23.45.

what is righteously desired. Human choice is not necessary, strictly speaking, to receive God's invitation but only to accept it, that is, scrupulously to obey its generous yet demanding terms.

The terms of God's invitation, however, were so exacting that natural powers were insufficient to sustain human will's loyal attempts to meet them. But, if only the person would pray for assistance beyond that which was received in the proper inclination of the will, will and ability would increase.[41] If no divine assistance were expected and actually forthcoming, God's first operation (*"De operante illo ut velimus"*), the invitation itself, would appear to be the sinister act of a creator who took perverse pleasure in his creatures' manifold frustrations.[42] But Augustine's God was both Creator and Redeemer, and, as Redeemer, God sent Christ and the Holy Spirit in order to break the bonds of human will's captivity.[43] The Holy Spirit confers growth in grace and perseverance upon wills that respond to God's invitation by participating in the expansion of their powers. The new human vitality that began with divine impetus is not arrested for want of God's continuing cooperation, because God keeps faith with the faith he inspires. Augustine therefore assured his readers of divine husbandry and nonetheless urged them to will and work their own salvation.

God and man were "co-workers." Augustine's assurances and exhortations lead to no other conclusion; and had he not mentioned it in the *De gratia et libero arbitrio*,[44] the thoughtful reader would have had to supply the notion of collaboration. This then was how Augustine came to express the lesson of his conversion. The achievement of the ability "to will by all means," commemorated in the eighth book of the *Confessions*, was the significant feature of an enduring conversion, but it was neither a purely human triumph over indecision nor simply a divine donation. The robust and righteous will was the product of divine inspiration and assistance and also the result of human effort.

If Augustine's early attestations presupposed God's care and human

---

[41]Ibid. 15.31.

[42]Ibid. 4.6.

[43]Ibid. 6.15.

[44]Ibid. 5.12.

collaboration, both clearly articulated in the *De gratia et libero arbitrio*, then at one level the discrepancy between the soteriology that preceded the Pelagian controversies and governed the writing of the *Confessions* and the soteriology that emerged from those controversies is more imaginary than real. In both instances, the effectiveness of grace and human willingness to become God's confederate were compatible and coefficient causes of a lasting conversion. Neither will nor grace alone could accomplish what God summons, inclines, and assists the faithful to accomplish in cooperation with him.

It is not altogether preposterous to suggest that Augustine equivo-cated in the *De gratia et libero arbitrio*: he renewed his attack on the Pelagians with sweeping declarations that God was the source of the righteous human will, and yet he borrowed the Pelagian argument that free choice in redemptive activity was sufficiently proven by a formidable array of biblical admonitions and commandments.[45] Notwithstanding the apparent equivocation, Augustine's treatise is actually a carefully quilted work in which the two sides of the soteriology have been stitched together and yet are held apart by a lining of subtle, though simple, statements which amount to an explanation of how we come to live righteously by faith.[46] God's mercy and grace precede human faith and works of righteousness proceed from faith. By faith, Augustine signified the beginning of a personal commitment, a beginning which must be ascribed to divine initiative. By righteous works, Augustine indicated voluntary obedience to scriptural counsels as well as charity and other fruits of divine inspiration and continued divine assistance without which no commitment would endure.

---

[45]Ibid., 7.17: "Gratia salvi facti estis per fidem, et hoc non ex vobis, sed Dei donum est. Possent enim dicere, Ideo accepimus gratiam, quia credidimus; tanquam sibi fidem tribuentes, gratiam Deo: propter hoc Apostolus cum dixisset, per fidem; et hoc, inquit, non ex vobis, sed Dei donum est." Also 2.2: "Revelavit autem nobis per Scripturas suas sanctas, esse in homine liberum voluntatis arbitrium. Quomodo autem revelaverit, com-memoro vos, non humano eloquio, sed divino. Primum, quia ipsa divina praecepta homini non prodessent, nisi haberet liberum voluntatis arbitrium, quo ea faciens ad promissa praemia perveniret."

[46]Ibid. 7.16-18; 12.24; 15.31; 18.37-39.

Augustine as Church Reformer?

Augustine's concern for personal righteousness was not unrelated to his position on church order. But travel from one set of propositions about the righteous will to another set about the righteous church required the utmost discretion and circumspection. Although worldliness and, in instances, wrongdoing threatened discipline and devotion, Augustine was prepared by the century that witnessed so much unpredictable change to labor for stability in institutional structure and policy even as he encouraged radical change in personal piety and loyalty.

Of course, the Bishop of Hippo attended diligently to individual scandals as they surfaced. His letters and sermons counsel prudence and charity that issue in progress in Christian perfection.[47] Next to Pelagian and Donatist protests and proclamations that pressed for doctrinal and structural reform, however, Augustine's notes on the morality of church life appear more managerial than reformist. Personal reform and righteousness seem to be one thing and institutional rehabilitation and organized morality, for Augustine, seem to be something altogether different. But this is deceptive. It is absolutely correct to judge that the connection between personal morality and institutional health was not as simple for Augustine as it was for the followers of Pelagius. It is also proper to record that Augustine's idealism was not as easily translated into institutional reorganization as was Donatist perfectionism. Augustine understood *reformatio* in terms of the personality. His *Confessions* spoke exclusively of character deformation and reformation, at one point associating personal reform with both divine prompting and the restless human search for salvation, in a fashion perfectly conformable with his later mention of collaboration.[48] "Correction, reformation of the human person," according to Gerhart Ladner, is Augustine's "sole remedy against the evils of history. . . . [T]he church exists truly in its saints."[49] Still, it would be unfair to repress the institutional ramification of Augus-

---

[47]See, for example, Augustine's letter to certain "sisters" of the convent in Hippo (*Epistle* 211.12), the letter customarily termed Augustine's "Rule."

[48]*Conf.* 7.8.12.

[49]Gerhart Ladner, *The Idea of Reform: Its Impact on Christian Thought and Action in the Age of the Fathers* (Cambridge, 1959), p. 279.

tine's idea of reform, an idea that involved not only the personal restoration of Adam's innocence but also increase in personal perfection and social well-being.

Personal perfection did not necessarily lead to institutional reorganization. Augustine highly regarded the *ecclesia* as the community of the faithful and righteous Christians, and he frequently identified it with the city of God.[50] But, as Wilhelm Kamlah noted, this neither endorsed nor directly challenged the prevailing structure of the institution. Augustine's identification chiefly denoted his appreciation for the community (*Gemeinde*) rather than his concern in any way with the hierarchy (*Kirche*).[51] Kamlah stressed the eschatological orientation of Augustine's equation between *ecclesia* (as *Gemeinde*) and *civitas Dei*, so it is useful to return to the *De civitate Dei*, Augustine's famous apology for "official" Christianity, and to sort through the Bishop's remarks in order to measure the extent to which the *ecclesia* was identified with the City, the assembled saints of past, present, and future. The question is one of survival, that is, the survival of Augustine's care for the life and reform of the institutional church, what Kamlah called the "empirical Catholic church," in the presence of his pronounced individualistic understanding of righteousness and reform (as per Ladner's observation) and in the face of his eschatological orientation. Fortunately, Etienne Gilson has done the required sorting, and his findings bear directly on this question of survival in two ways. The church, for Augustine, was only part of the city of God. More explicitly, it was the part in pilgrimage in time, the imperfect token of the consummation of personal righteousness in some future communion of the elect and blessed.[52] Imperfection, however, did

---

[50]See, inter alia, *Ennar. in Ps.* 98.4; and *De civ. Dei* 8.24 and 14.2.

[51]Wilhelm Kamlah, *Christentum und Geschichtlichkeit: Untersuchungen zur Entstehung des Christentums und zu Augustins "Bürgerschaft Gottes,"* (Frankfurt, 1940), pp. 175-76. In Kamlah's judgment, increasing emphasis upon the *sacerdotium* during the Middle Ages pushed laypersons from the pages of ecclesiology and promoted the equation between *ecclesia* and hierarchy. (But see, in this connection, Hubert Jedin, "Mittelalterliche Wurzeln des Klerikalismus," *Kirche des Glaubens—Kirche der Geschichte*, I [Freiburg, 1966], pp. 331-45.) Kamlah complains that the equation is still influential in studies of Augustine's ecclesiology. His own persuasive reshuffling of terminology is adopted here.

[52]Etienne Gilson, "Eglise et cité de Dieu," *Archives d'histoire doctrinale et littéraire du Moyen Age* 20 (1953): 20-22.

not mean insignificance. The pilgrim church was a prefiguration of the *regnum Christi*, and its proper administration must be a matter of theological as well as practical concern. Also the notion of pilgrimage invites one to think of movement, preferably growth, if not in numbers then in harmony and unity, growth that then constitutes the institutional consequence of personal reform. Augustine reproached the Donatists for their intolerance of imperfection and for their expectation for the sudden reorganization of church life. He was not unsympathetic with their preoccupation with discipline, but he associated church reform with the institution's pilgrimage: reform was a continuous and subtle affair, as was the soul's salvation, abetted by God's secret assistance rather than implemented, all at once, according to human and therefore limited understandings of morality.

This did not suggest to Augustine the total inapplicability of moral theology, more precisely, of moral standards within the church. They were formulated and applied with too much urgency and finality by Donatists: the evil will remain within the church through the whole course of its earthly pilgrimage (*"quamdiu peregrinatur in mundo"*).[53] The ultimate separation of good from evil must await history's end. Continuous reformation, personal and, by extension, institutional, was not similarly delayed. Evil will remain within the church, but its force may be restrained and diminished and it must surely be kept from power and privilege in the institution. The year after his ordination, Augustine wrote to his bishop, Valerius, and he requested that councils be called to promote widespread reform of clerical conduct.[54] Persons, who may prescribe well for others but who betray by their behavior disrespect for their own prescriptions, were as citizens of Babylon administering Jerusalem.[55] Had Augustine's energies not been absorbed by his contests with would-be reformers who modified accepted doctrine or traditional structure to get the desired result of a disciplined, moral church life, his own reformation based on personal righteousness might have achieved

---

[53]*De civ. Dei* 1.35.

[54]*Epistle* 22.2.

[55]*Ennar. in Ps.* 61.8. This indictment found an echo in virtually each successive generation, and it becomes the characteristic accusation of late medieval Catholic reform.

greater success once he replaced Valerius.

If it had appeared to Augustine that the silence of Pelagians and Donatists could be purchased at a smaller price in his time and energy, we would know far more about the Bishop's ecclesiology and perhaps we might possess sufficient evidence to evaluate him as a reformer. But his efforts, such as they were, to relate righteousness to church reform do show the place and importance of the one true church in the sweep of his soteriology. Within the church persons receive fully God's grace. Sacraments administered by schismatics, though not absolutely invalid, were unable to deliver the abundance of God's gifts and assistance, and Augustine came to encourage the use of coercive measures to dislodge persons from one "church" and return them to the other but true church that struggled for the complete redemption of its members with divine approval and aid and therefore with the hope of eternal peace.[56]

Peculiar structural innovations in church government and formal alterations in worship and discipline often unnecessarily restricted the struggle for righteousness. Augustine advised that, inasmuch as customs will vary, the wise Christian should conform to local practice in things objectionable neither to faith nor to morals.[57] One might consider his ecclesiology "institutionally minimal," because the real issue for him was personal motivation, *caritas*, and its practical expression in spirituality and service. The church, where discipline and devotion gradually and

---

[56]To justify the use of "merciful violence" in the retrieval of schismatics, Augustine in 417 summoned his considerable rhetorical skill. See his letter to Boniface, then governor of Africa (*Epistle* 185.32): "Quorum si videas in Christi pace laetitias, frequentias, alacritates et ad hymnos audiendos et canendos et ad verbum dei percipiendum celebres hilaresque conventus multorumque in eis cum dolore magno recordationem praeteriti erroris et cum gaudio considerationem cognitae veritatis et cum indignatione et detestatione mendacium magistrorum, quod modo cognoscant, de nostris sacramentis quam falsa iactuerint, multorum etiam in eis confessiones, quod olim vellent esse catholici nec inter homines tanti furoris auderent, horum ergo populorum congregationes per plurimas Africae regiones ab illa perditione liberatorum si sub uno conspectu videres, tunc diceres nimiae fuisse crudelitatis, si, dum timeretur, ne homines desperati et istorum innumerabili multitudini nulla aestimatione comparandi suis et voluntariis ignibus cremarentur, isti in aeternum perdendi et sempiternis ignibus cruciandi relinquerentur."

[57]*Epistle* 54.2: "Quod enim neque contra fidem neque contra bonos mores esse convincitur, indifferenter habendum et pro eorum, inter quos vivitur, societate servandum est."

continuously expelled worldliness from the personal and corporate lives of its members, was the setting for constant reform, the place for constant progress in perfection, and in Charles Brockwell's words, a "laboratory of love," where details of structure were clearly of secondary importance.[58] Charity, the culmination of divine and human collaboration in personal reform and righteousness, and unity, the reflection of God's order in the church, were inseparable.[59] Consistently with the principles of his soteriology, Augustine refused to legislate, with the precision desired by his contemporaries and often supplied by his heirs, the ongoing work of God in the *reformatio* of his faithful and in the reform of his church. To know, however, that the work was authored similarly by God and by man is to understand Augustine's thinking on personal righteousness and church reform.

---

[58]See Charles W. Brockwell, Jr., "Augustine's Ideal of Monastic Community: A Paradigm for His Doctrine of the Church," *Augustinian Studies* 8 (1977): 108.

[59]*Epistle* 61.2.

An Augustinian Tradition
in the Twelfth Century

The Idea of Collaboration in an Age of Compilation

Theological advances during the early Middle Ages are difficult to measure. Various collations of venerable opinions and abridgments of texts responded more to the practical needs of episcopal government than to possibilities for speculative understanding present in theological reflection. Caught in the turbulence of early European politics and jeopardized by barbarian invasions, the churches required ready access to some ancient consensus as a matter of self-interpretation and survival. Compilations served that purpose, and compilers worked with increasing sophistication during and after the Carolingian period. Practical exigencies, however, customarily held the speculative imagination of the Western church to such tasks as the clarification of the sacramental system and the investigation of warrants for papal and episcopal prerogatives. Papal authority was especially and scrupulously analyzed as the investiture controversy heated in the eleventh century.[1]

Piety and personal holiness, of course, were topics of interest, and compilers frequently appropriated Augustine's terminology, especially with reference to the identifications of grace *operans, cooperans, adiu-*

---

[1] J. de Ghellinck, *Le Mouvement théologique du XII siècle*, 2nd ed. (Bruges, 1948), pp. 1-9, 52-65.

vans, perseverans, and the like.[2] The language of Augustine, however, appears to have been chosen and adapted with some indifference to Augustine's own understanding of grace and will before the time of Anselm of Canterbury, Bernard of Clairveaux, and Peter Lombard. Augustine's meaning was often obscured or lost in the bushels of texts and quotations with which compilers addressed the problems of their times. This as well as the dominant concern with practical issues in church government accounts for the difficulties one encounters when speaking of theological advance and perhaps also for the immense popularity and influence of Peter Lombard's at once detailed and profound *Libri sententiarum.*

By the twelfth century the problem of resolving apparent contradictions in the opinions collected from venerable texts became acute. This was no small tribute to the increasing sensitivity with which the early medieval compilers and collators did their work. But this fact did little to mitigate the embarrassment or to rescue consensus from the reigning confusion. The task of harmonization was complicated by the notion that God's infallible Spirit had moved Church Fathers to make their pronouncements and had indeed shaped the very pronouncements that seemed to contradict one another. Compilers and codifiers of canonical legislation might plead the influence of changing circumstances and contexts, but in matters of doctrine it was no easy matter to concede the obsolescence of certain opinions or to explain the differences between Augustine and Chrysostom and at the same time to prevent skepticism with reference to the universality and truthfulness of Christian teaching.[3]

Two avenues opened for the twelfth-century theologian. Ever since Berengar of Tours toward the end of the eleventh century subjected certain components of faith to critical examination, the career of reason in theology seemed assured. The prospect of solving doctrinal problems and eliminating contradiction with dialectic was irresistible to some who decided to plot a course through the tangle of conflicting pronouncements. Others unravelled the relationships between experience and reas-

[2]Artur Michael Landgraf, *Dogmengeschichte der Frühscholastik,* 1.1 (Regensburg, 1952), pp. 51-53.

[3]See de Ghellinck, *Le Mouvement théologique,* pp. 474-78.

onable inference and between reason and the mysteries of faith without direct concern for discordant opinions. Their course passed over, so to speak, the conflicts between authorities, although it did not avoid the conflicts of the twelfth century. To some considerable extent, these contemporary conflicts arose because the foremost protagonists of each approach attempted more or less successfully to reach and to reclaim the solutions earlier endorsed by Augustine.

Peter Abelard's compendious *Sic et non* outshines all other twelfth-century efforts to dramatize discordances. But Abelard selected from the broad expanse of Augustine's soteriology remarks that simplified his predecessor's anthropology. Abelard's investigation of the proposition *"Quod bonam voluntatem nostram gratia praecedit"* is representative. He used Augustine to confirm that nothing was attributable to human action inasmuch as God's grace preceded human involvement and inclined human will so that the Christian might then wish for the best. Abelard's exposition of the *et contra* repeated John Chrysostom's opinion that it was the province of human will to desire and to choose the good and the province of divine will to perfect that choice. Unlike Anselm of Canterbury before him and Bernard of Clairveaux after and perhaps in reaction to him, Abelard did not elect to examine the delicate balance between grace and free will. This may account for the fact that he was seen to have favored each of the two opposing sides of the proposition and that the *"Errores Petri Abaelard"* condemned at the Council of Sens (1140) scolded him for apparently Pelagian *and* dogmatically un-Pelagian positions. But it must be understood that the very character of his doctrinal sourcebook prohibited him from reconciling the ostensibly antithetical arguments. In the *Sic et non* Augustine remained merely one side of the dialectic.[4]

One should have expected Abelard, as the alleged champion of inquiry over authority, to have grasped at other opportunities to reconcile substantial differences of opinion. His notion that harmonization might depend upon the recognition of the various significations used by differ-

---

[4]See Abelard's *Sic et non* 139; and *Enchiridion symbolorum definitionum et declarationum de rebus fidei et morum*, ed. Heinrich Denzinger, 11th ed. (Freiburg, 1911), pp. 273 and 280.

ent authors to explain the same word held great promise for the manipulation of discrepancies and the recovery of consensus.[5] With respect to grace and will, however, Abelard in his exposition of Romans relied upon a peculiarly unsubtle appropriation of the Augustine of his *Sic et non*. Divine compassion was not simply the perfection of that which was freely desired and chosen, as it had been for Chrysostom, but rather was a prevenient force that converted the unwilling person. Inclination of the will was indeed a prelude to redemptive works, but Abelard commended Augustine for his confirmation that the profitable inclination owed its existence to divine will. This does much to vitiate the enigmatic bipartisanship of the *Sic et non*. But it also testifies to Abelard's failure to make much of Augustine's more complex position. The course plotted through the maze of competing authorities, in this instance, underscored the disparity between them.[6] It was left to Peter Lombard to use Augustine as an agent of reconciliation.

Abelard may have appropriated Augustine's most severe statements about human impotence in order to stress the problem of reconciliation and to prepare in the *Sic et non* the case for inquiry and dialectic. Still, his exposition of Romans, apparently without hesitation, sponsored a rather uncompromising interpretation of those statements, perhaps to salvage his reputation in more "orthodox" circles. Peter Lombard applied himself to the same problems of reconciliation and orthodoxy or consensus. Indispensable for his work and, in part, responsible for his success was the deeper understanding of Augustine's soteriology provided by theologians who had acquired a certain proficiency in restoring Augustine's thought without demonstrable preoccupation with other competing assessments of the respective roles of grace and human will.

The final section of the *De concordia praescientiae et praedestinationis et gratiae Dei cum libero arbitrio*, the last of Anselm of Canterbury's major works, was devoted to the establishment of the proper relationship between grace and free choice. Anselm explained that free will was necessary to secure the aptitude for righteousness without which human will remained soteriologically ineffective. Once God contributed upright-

---

[5] *Expositio in epistola Pauli ad Romanos*, "Prologus," PL 178: 1344D.
[6] Ibid., Book 1, PL 178: 825C; and Book 4, PL 178: 914D-915A.

ness, human will, assisted by subsequent grace, persevered so as to evoke still further divine assistance. Human will, which restlessly and impotently longs for righteousness, collaborates with grace, which ab initio bestows the capacity or disposition for righteousness and thereafter increases the will's power to hold fast to and grow in righteousness.[7]

Anselm's debts to Augustine have often been acknowledged. But it has been common practice to ascribe greatest significance to grace as the necessary precondition for the gift and the safekeeping of uprightness and to forget the will's "hypothetical" freedom, the longing for righteousness, that precedes the restoration of the disposition for righteousness and, actualized by that restoration, collaborates with grace. The restoration, according to Anselm, reflected God's pardon. Furnished with the disposition for righteousness and strengthened by subsequent grace, human will might freely and steadfastly choose righteousness for its own sake and therefore might become worthy of the divine pardon and worthy of beatitude.[8]

Anselm was convinced that divine grace pervaded the entire redemptive process. Drawing upon St. Paul's agrarian imagery in I Corinthians, he asserted that God not only planted the seed of righteousness but also supervised and actually "gave" growth (*"incrementum dat Deus"*).[9] He did not, as has been alleged, so "hypostasize" uprightness that the role of grace would be limited to the provision of the will with its proper object.[10] Nor did Anselm altogether proscribe human will and its longing for righteousness, which remained even after the disposition for righteousness had disappeared. The will's natural condition included an untested and therefore "hypothetical" freedom. This ordinary but cramped and desperate state became an extraordinary power when rectitude gripped

---

[7]*De concordia* 3.3, in *S. Anselmi Cantuariensis Archiepiscopi opera omnia*, ed. Franciscus Salesius Schmitt, 6 vols. (Seckau and Edinburgh, 1938-1961) 2:265-67.

[8]Consult my "Confirmation of Augustine's Soteriology: Human Will's Collaboration with Divine Grace according to Anselm of Canterbury," *Mediaevalia* 4 (1978): 147-60.

[9]*De concordia* 3.6, in Schmitt (ed.), *S. Anselmi*, 2:270-71.

[10]Cf. Jaspar Hopkins, *A Companion to the Study of St. Anselm* (Minneapolis, 1972), pp. 155-58. But also note Philippe Delhaye, "Quelques aspects de la morale de Saint Anselme," *Spicilegium Beccense* 1 (1959): 414-15; and Robert Pouchet, *La rectitude chez saint Anselme* (Paris, 1964), pp. 33-44.

the will and, in turn, enabled the will to hold fast and to exercise its freedom. Anselm's modest concession to volition's place in soteriology was entirely consonant with Augustine's. Neither theologian exhaustively detailed the collaboration between grace and will. But readers familiar with the general processes by which grace has made it impossible to will by all means (Augustine) and "to keep righteousness for its own sake" (Anselm) are also familiar, as if their eyes had grown accustomed to a comfortable and perhaps comforting darkness, with the vague outlines of a mysteriously apportioned synergism.

The real danger of oversimplifying this "obscure subject" may have led Bernard of Clairveaux, with whom Peter Lombard was acquainted, to extrapolate from his own experience of God's grace. Speculations offered especially in the sixth chapter of his *De gratia et libero arbitrio* correspond well with the wisdom of Augustine and Anselm. He admitted that human will's power, the gift of *creans gratia*, was nonetheless powerless for good, if unsupported by saving grace. But will was not idle. As was St. Paul ("I can will what is right, but I cannot do it"—Romans 7:18), each individual was engaged in what must be, without divine assistance, a futile struggle. To will the good effectively was the achievement of both human volition and divine grace, not necessarily in sequence but, according to Bernard, in collaboration so intimate that the will's conversion may be said to have been both a divine work and a human choice.[11]

Peter Lombard and the Shape of Voluntarist Mysticism

The daring initiative of Anselm and the scheme that Bernard abstracted from his experience, along with collections of doctrine and canon law such as Abelard's compendium, influenced Peter Lombard not only as he composed his *Sentences* but also, previous to that, as he wrote his commentaries on the Psalms and on Paul's letters. His speculative and exegetical work covered the whole field of soteriology as comprehensively as any of his immediate predecessors had, but Peter's approach to

---

[11]*De gratia et libero arbitrio* 18, in *Sancti Bernardi opera* 3 (Rome, 1963), p. 179, lines 15-20: "Ceterum sive Dei sumus, sive diaboli, non tamen similiter desinimus esse et nostri. Manet quippe utrobique libertas arbitrii, per quam maneat et causa meriti, quatenus merito vel puniamur mali, quod tamquam liberi ex propria voluntate efficimur, vel glorificemur boni, quod nisi aeque voluntarii esse non possumus."

certain issues was slightly different from either of the two discussed thus far. He was conscious that frequently cited authorities were not infrequently at odds with one another, but he was not at all confident that harmonization was a matter of logic. He was prepared to leave dialecticians to their own devices and to look behind the history of more recent quarrels and confusions to the early acts of the Christian drama. Precedent for dismissing "garruli ratiocinatores," as well as the resolution of thorny soteriological questions was to be had in Augustine's writing, and Peter Lombard remained more steadfastly and perceptibly attached to Augustine than had either Anselm or Bernard.[12] He learned more from Augustine of the mysterious collaboration between God's sovereign grace and the active yet debilitated human will. This lesson, in contradistinction to the more complex codifications of putatively Augustinian *Gnadenlehren* that subsequently demystified the mechanics of grace's operations and the inner connections between grace and human will, stands as a monument to Augustine's synergism and voluntaristic mysticism.[13]

Consideration of Peter's lesson and the easy recognition of Augustine's place there involve first setting in its proper perspective twelfth-century talk of merit, which so upset later church reformers and their historians of dogma,[14] and then relating the colaboration of grace and will to righteousness in the context of Peter Lombard's work.

---

[12]See de Ghellinck, *Le Mouvement théologique*, pp. 229-30.

[13]Ferdinand Cavallera agrees that the case for Augustine's overwhelming influence is a persuasive one, but his validation amounts to little more than counting and measuring citations in the *Libri sententiarum*. His figures nonetheless are noteworthy. Consult his "Saint Augustin et le Livre des Sentences de Pierre Lombard," *Archives de philosophie* 7 (1930):186-99.

[14]John Calvin's charges against Peter are perhaps the most familiar. Calvin was astonished that Peter ostensibly kept Augustine constantly in mind and yet so misinterpreted him on the question of merit (*Institutes* 3.15.7). Of course, this presumed a vastly different reading of Peter's position than the one offered here, but it also relied upon a considerably strict construction of Augustine's anti-Pelagian polemics that precluded the notion of collaboration (2.3.7, 11, and 13). Calvin distinguished between the schoolmen for whom he had nothing but contempt and the few, more sober and yet fundamentally in error, who were greeted with comparatively mild disapprobation and among whom Peter was numbered (2.2.6). But Peter, according to Calvin, was far less faithful than Bernard to Augustine's understanding of human freedom (2.3.5). Also note Adolf Harnack's reproduction of the "Semi-Pelagian ring" of Peter's alleged modification of Augustinianism, *History of Dogma*, trans. Neil Buchanan, vol. 6 (New York, 1961), pp. 276-81.

The classification of human unrighteousness, that is, works that precede justifying faith, was no simple or superfluous matter for the twelfth century. Lest, through some misunderstanding, the apostle's authority (Romans 14:23: "Whatever does not proceed from faith is sin") were taken to proscribe altogether the good works of unbelievers, Anselm of Laon, Simon of Tournai, and Gilbert of Poitiers, to name but a few, insisted that "sin," in this instance, merely signified works valueless with reference to salvation.[15] These works might well be virtuous, but insofar as they were accomplished without justifying faith, they were not meritorious.[16] Some argued that such works were necessary and might be imagined as a preliminary species of righteousness. All, save Gilbert and his followers, however, conceded that an unmerited infusion of grace preceded the good works of unbelievers. Gilbert contended that the first infusion of grace followed the remission of sins, and this suggested that some form of faith was acquired without grace.[17] It would be sensible to expect that the whole range of issues raised by Gilbert's dissent would have exhausted talk of merit, but this is not even remotely accurate. The twelfth century in general,[18] and Peter Lombard in particular,[19] referred the question and possibility of merit to the believer's worthiness for an increase of grace and for beatitude.

There is nothing exceptional about Peter's claim that a person might be deserving of divine compassion. His appeal to the Pseudo-Augustine's

---

[15]See Landgraf, *Dogmengeschichte der Frühscholastik* 1.1:59-60.

[16]Ibid., 1.1:287-90.

[17]See Artur Michael Landgraf, "Untersuchungen zu den Eigenlehren Gilberts de la Porée," *Zeitschift für katholische Theologie* 54 (1930): 180-213.

[18]See Landgraf, *Dogmengeschichte der Frühscholastik* 1.1:200-201. Henri Rondet applied a deceptively simple formula to Anselm's discussion of merit and subsequent graces: "en coopérant à la grâce, la volonté mérite un accroissement de grâce, des forces pour persévérer, enfin une récompense." See Rondet's "Grâce et péché l'Augustinisme de Saint Anselme," *Spicilegium Beccense* 1 (1959): 168; but observe also that the formula is valid only if "merit" indicates proof that the will was worthy of growth in grace. Anselm clearly contended that the restoration of righteousness, continual assistance, and growth in grace toward the final goal were given by God. Human "merit," then, does not compel divine reward. Certain expectations aroused by the use of the term are symptomatic of a later age of interpretation, not of the twelfth century.

[19]See Johann Schupp, *Die Gnadenlehre des Petrus Lombardus* (Freiburg, 1932), pp. 95-105.

treatise on penance in his own discussion of contrition is representative of his position in the *Sentences*.

> Consider if one is worthy of mercy. I do not say of justice; justice only condemns. But one who seeks grace with his spiritual labors, whose courage endures shame, deserves mercy. Inasmuch as great modesty is expiation, whoever endures shame for Christ is made worthy of God's mercy. It is therefore clear that the more he will confess the infamy of his evildoing in the hope of indulgence, the more easily the grace of remission will follow.[20]

It would be hard to reconstruct this passage to support unambiguously Gilbert's notion that meritorious works preceded the infusion of a first grace. Shame and remorse are "spiritual labors." They occur after God's pardon has been received as promise and they are dedicated to Christ (*"qui erubescit pro Christo, fit dignus misericordia"*). They are not then acts *de genere bonorum*, but rather they constitute a penance undertaken in the context of Christian faith and (Peter did not use the adjective "spiritual" carelessly) with the assistance of, indeed, in the presence of the Holy Spirit. Only in this mode are these labors meritorious.

Unless the place of "spiritual labors" in Peter's soteriology is restored in this fashion, and upon such a restoration my own argument rests, the second book of his *Sentences*, seasoned with anti-Pelagian declarations, makes little sense.[21] The assumption that a first grace might be earned by human will's industry in the pursuit of good perceptibly distressed Peter, who was not above challenging his favorite theologian when he supposed him to have failed in precluding that possibility. He plainly disapproved

---

[20]*Libri sententiarum* 4.d.17.3 (quoting the Pseudo-Augustine's *De vera et falsa poenitentia* 10.25): "Considerat enim, si dignus est, non dico justitia, sed et misericordia; justitia enim sola damnat, sed dignus est misericordia qui spirituali labore quaerit gratiam: laborat enim mens patiendo erubescentiam; et quoniam verecundia magna est poena, qui erubescit pro Christo, fit dignus misericordia. Unde patet, quia, quanto pluribus confitebitur in spe veniae turpitudinem criminis, tanto facilius consequitur gratiam remissionis."

[21]Ibid., 2.d.28.1: "Praedicta repetit ut alia addat, definitam assignationem ponens de gratia et libero arbitrio contra Pelagianos. Id vero inconcusse et incunctanter teneamus, liberum arbitrium sine gratia praeveniente et adiuvante non sufficere ad iustitiam et salutem obtinendam, nec meritis praecedentibus gratiam Dei advocari, sicut Pelagiana haeresis tradidit. Nam ut ait Augustinus in I libro *Retractationum,* 'novi haeretici Pelagiani liberum sic asserunt voluntatis arbitrium, ut gratiae Dei non relinquant locum: quam secundum merita nostra dari asserunt."

of passages in Augustine's early works that appeared to corroborate Pelagian claims. Still, he awarded Augustine the last word, and he reiterated Augustine's *Retractationes* with such regularity that the Bishop of Hippo could be considered the author of several of his articles.[22] Peter emphatically noted that the first grace was unmerited. He contended that at every stage in the acquisition of *"libertas gratiae"* grace itself was operative, preparing, assisting, and perfecting human will.[23]

Was this symptomatic of some decline in Peter's faith in human will? The *Libri sententiarum* boast a profound respect for the versatility and constant presence of grace, yet earlier exegetical work displays Peter's readiness to assign a significant, if uncertain, role to human choice in the achievement of salvation. In Philippians 3:8-9 St. Paul discounted human righteousness, but Peter's commentary deferred to Augustine's proclamation that justification involves some participation of the justified (*"qui te fecit sine te, non te justificat sine te"*).[24] Rather than relinquish his position, he deftly advanced it in the face of the strongest of the apostle's remarks to the contrary, Romans 9:16 ("it depends not upon man's will"). Peter suggested that God's mercy counted nothing without human will.[25] Hence the words *"non est volentis"* indicated only that nothing good comes of efforts unprepared by grace.[26] Salvation was not exclusively or primarily attributable to human choice, but human will was dimly perceived by Peter as a force of order in the pursuit of righteousness, and human effort was presumed to have a direct bearing on the success or failure of God's visitation. Peter carefully explained that this had nothing whatsoever to do with merit. It must not be said that one was justified *"per propriam voluntatem."* But Peter added, without fanfare and yet with sufficient stress to complicate the issue, that justification could not be said to proceed *"sine voluntate nostra."*[27]

Johann Schupp's valuable dissertation on Peter's *Gnadenlehre*

---

[22]E.g., ibid., 2.d.28.3.

[23]Ibid., 2.d.25.9.

[24]*Collectanea in epist. d. Pauli*, PL 192: 245B.

[25]Ibid., PL 191: 1461A.

[26]Ibid., PL 191: 1460D.

[27]Ibid., PL 191: 1361C.

implied that the *Sentences* atoned with omissions and qualifications for Peter's earlier indiscretion.[28] Far from signaling an erosion of the initial position, however, Peter's mature work sharpened and extended it. He repeated Augustine's stipulation that the Christian was not justified "*sine voluntate*," and that notion formed an affirmation central to the second book of the *Sentences*.[29] Free choice, a power ("*facultas*") of both reason and will, could elect the good, "*gratia assistente*." Indeed, "*sine libero arbitrio*," virtue would not be translated into act and therefore righteousness. But, "*gratia desistente*," the will, though free, was necessarily delinquent.[30]

Human will runs afoul because it is powerless, and the sum and substance of grace's assistance, be it preparing, aiding, or perfecting, is empowerment. Human will's part, however, is more difficult to determine. Anselm located it with the will's aptitude for righteousness, and Peter may have had this premise in mind when he reconstructed Augustine's position from the *Retractationes*. He judged that Augustine had correctly assigned the aptitude for faith and love ("*posse habere*") to human nature and the actual possession of faith and love ("*habere*") to grace.[31] But ironically, Peter came closest to the sense of Augustine's voluntarism when he was not absorbed in the transcription of the *Retractationes*, Augustine's most mature yet frankly apologetic remarks.

Augustinian conceptions of spirituality and of human will are considerably tamed by references to aptitudes and dispositions. To recover Augustine's meaning, human will must be understood in terms of "*concupiscentia*," its inept yearning for freedom and righteousness; and that yearning should be understood as the will's collaboration with God, who prepares it for righteousness. Peter integrated both understandings with his account of human will's part in justification. He specified that a person must want to believe and to hope but that God must prepare the will for such salutary desires. Some portion of human assent ("*vult credere*") appears to precede faith, but God's gift of faith accompanies the

---

[28]Schupp, *Die Gnadenlehre des Petrus*, pp. 114-15, 155-59, 203-206.

[29]*Libri sententiarum* 2.d.27.1.

[30]Ibid., 2.d.24.3 and d.27.6.

[31]Ibid., 2.d.28.3.

process of assent and may be said to precede it, "*non tempore, sed causa et natura*."[32] Earlier Peter reviewed the somewhat complex relationship between longing ("*concupiscentia*") and desire ("*desiderium*").

> Longing is desire, but the two are not identical. Longing pertains to things that are possessed as well as to things that are not. Desire pertains only to those things absent from this life. Note then that [the Psalmist, 119:20] says, "he longed to desire"; he does not say that he desired [God's ordinances]. Sometimes we realize the usefulness of God's ordinances, that is, of *opera justitiae*, but because of our weakness we do not desire them.[33]

Longing is a foundational and apparently unfocused aspiration. It is a yearning after a derivative but far more focused feeling. It might be called the primordial element in humanity's assent to grace, although pride of place is usually given to some acquired intelligence of the good. For Peter, "*concupiscentia*," as a movement of free choice occasioned by God but not, strictly speaking, by grace, begins the pursuit of righteousness. To the degree that this longing conflated divine and human wills, it conformed to the classification of preliminary righteousness introduced by Peter's predecessors and it conforms with the notion of "broad penance" suggested by some of his successors and students.[34] More important still, Peter's discussions of human assent recall Augustine's discernment of his own longing and of the process by which grace enabled him to will by all means.

The process of justification, culminating in righteousness, was a composite of human assent, divine operation, and divine cooperation. The latter two divisions were set forth in Augustine's *De gratia et libero arbitrio* in a formula that prevailed through the Middle Ages and burned

---

[32]Ibid., 2.d.26.4-6.

[33]*Commentarium in Psalmos*, PL 191: 1055A-B: "Et nota quod concupiscentia est desiderium, sed non omnis, quia concupiscentia est et eorum quae habentur, et eorum quae non habentur. Desiderium vero absentium tantum est in hac vita. Nota etiam quod ait: 'Concupivit disiderare,' non ait desideravit. Videmus enim ratione nonnunquam quam utiles sunt justificationes Dei, id est opera justitiae sed infirmitate aliquando non desideramus." Also review the distinction between longing and desire in Augustine's discussion of the same psalm, *Enarratio in psalmum CXVIII*, PL 37: 1522.

[34]See Landgraf, *Dogmengeschichte der Frühscholastik* 1.1:299-300.

its insignia into the soteriologies of his heirs. Peter used it to preface his own explanation of free choice. God's cooperation perfects in us that which his operation began. The beginning is prior to the will's achievement of goodness. Indeed the virtue of which human will, *gratia assistente*, makes good use is an unmerited divine gift. Despite human longing, itself a divinely moved preparation, the beginning is wholly attributable to God. This is true because the actual prosecution of good works, for Augustine and for Peter Lombard, requires liberation as well as preparation. Divine grace confers liberation, assistance, efficiency, and ultimately perfection. Taken together with divine operation in human assent, this was an explanation of empowerment but also an illustration of how the prepared, liberated, and assisted will collaborated in God's work.[35]

"Illustration" is probably too strong a word for the glimpses afforded by Peter's recasting of Augustine's soteriology. The *Libri sententiarum* and the exegetical work do not disclose the entire constitution of the process of justification, but they separate certain "moments" in that process sufficiently to allow a pattern to appear. God's prevenient work prepares human will with a discernible but ineffectual longing to desire the good. This leads to human assent to the summons of grace, but human will cannot actually desire the good until divine operation achieves its liberation and implants the virtues of faith and charity. Divine cooperation makes it possible not only to will but also to do the good. Something must be said, however, to prevent students from approaching this pattern with unbecoming solemnity. Peter Lombard did not formulate an exact science of grace. He spoke reverently of divine inscrutability, and he esteemed the abiding mystery of God's saving communication with created spirits.[36] This is nowhere more obvious than in Peter's remarks about the special relationship between the Holy Spirit and the human soul. St. Paul's confidence in this relationship (Romans 8:16, "*Ipse enim Spiritus testimonium reddit spiritui nostro quod sumus filii Dei*") was

---

[35]See Augustine's *De gratia et libero arbitrio* 17.33; and Peter's *Libri sententiarum* 2.d.26.1-2 and d.27.7.

[36]See, for example, *Commentarium in psalmos*, PL 191: 960B-C and *Collectanea in epist. D. Pauli*, PL 192: 193A-B.

renewed unequivocally in succeeding generations, but that *"testimonium"* was subjected to the strictest surveillance after the proscription of Aristotelian natural philosophy and metaphysics was revoked in 1255 by the Faculty of Arts at the University of Paris. Before the partnership between St. Paul and Aristotle was effectively contracted, however, the apostle's confidence was explained in Augustinian terms, and only by unfair comparison to later exploitation of the Stagarite's categories do those explanations appear vague and ontologically unsophisticated. A century before the Paris rehabilitation of Aristotle's reputation, Peter identified the spiritual communication with the *remissio peccatorum* in his own commentary on Romans 8:16.

> Although the Trinity effects this remission, it is understood properly as the Holy Spirit's work because the Spirit is common to Father and Son and to their union through which comes that unity and harmony by which we are made one body of God's only begotten son. The unity made by love joins us together, and there is no love, save from the Holy Spirit. Therefore, the Spirit gives life. It makes alive only those whom it finds in the body that it quickens just as the human spirit does not give life to a member found separated from the body. All this is mentioned so that we might love union and fear separation.[37]

Two things are especially noteworthy here. First, Peter closely associated the work of the Spirit with the unity of the church, and this association, wholly Augustinian, will figure prominently in the discussion of righteousness and church reform. More important for the present consideration of Peter's interpretation of Augustine's soteriology is his identification of love with the Spirit's communication and work, a noble and traditional equation that is central to his contemplation of an exalted piety.

---

[37]*Collectanea in epist. D. Pauli,* PL 191: 1440D-1441A: "Quam remissionem cum Trinitas faciat, proprie tamen ad Spiritum sanctum intelligitur pertinere, quia Spiritus communis est Patri et Filio, ambrorumque unio, per quem fit societas et unitas, qua efficimur unum corpus unici Filii Dei. Unitas enim nos compaginat, quem facit charitas, et charitas non est nisi a Spiritu sancto. Ergo spiritus est qui vivificat, quia viva facit membra nec viva facit, nisi quae in corpore quod vegetat invenerit, sicut spiritus hominis non vivificat membrum, quod separatum invenerit a corpore. Haec dicuntur ut amemus unitatem, et timeamus separationem." Also consult Schupp, *Die Gnadenlehre des Petrus,* pp. 216-31.

Peter's emphasis upon the church and its role in mediating the Spirit is neither unexpected nor extraordinary. Continuing debate about the prerogatives of the Pope and about the validity of sacraments administered by simoniacs gave few indications that agreement could be reached in the one short century following the great investiture controversies. Still, the importance of the church for the spiritual *"testimonium"* promised by St. Paul was uniformly recognized. Peter held that God created the church for the elect and then led them to it. Believers, however, must enter and approach "the higher and invisible altar," *"quo non accedit aliquis injustus."*[38] Their approach involves purification and reanimation of the soul, and this directly involves the sacraments with the establishment of the special relationship formed between the Holy and the human spirits. The fourth book of Peter's *Sentences* incorporates his concern for personal righteousness, which is achieved with this special relationship, in his theology of the sacraments. As Augustine before him, Peter seems to have forsaken that concern with his uninhibited confirmation that sacraments administered by an unworthy priest were nonetheless valid.[39] Part of the Augustinian theology of sacramental grace, this confirmation served to drown out the constant drumming of Donatist complaints with an affirmation of the sovereignty of grace. It only slightly disrupted the rhythm of Peter's thought, that is, his dedication to elaborate the apostle's confidence, *"Spiritus testimonium reddit spiritui nostro,"* in the terms of personal righteousness.

More need not be said of Peter's association of righteousness and spirituality with church order and sacramental grace. His notions of the grace and work of the Holy Spirit and of the significance of love and piety in the *ordo salutis* more boldly advanced Augustine's understandings of grace and will, and they therefore require greater attention.

Peter's few detailed expositions of the empowerment accomplished by grace tend to obscure St. Paul's confidence in a relatively simple spiritual communication. For example, Peter's exegesis of Psalm 23 released a multitude of graces, purportedly essential for the Christian's conversion, regeneration, and nourishment. Grace in baptism restores

---

[38]*Commentarium in psalmos*, PL 191: 426A.

[39]*Libri sententiarum* 4.d.19.2.

integrity to the soul ("He leads me beside still waters") The grace of restoration enlarges human virtues and sanctifies human efforts ("He leads me in the path of righteousness"), but yet another grace protects against distractions ("I fear no evil, for thou art with me"). Peter continued to match graces to virtues; although alongside later and systematic attempts to identify and organize graces and effects of grace, Peter's experiment seems fanciful and weightless. His terminology was inexact, and it dramatized the need for codification instead of furnishing a helpful model for classification. The more scientific intelligence of the next century has few roots in the Lombard's thought, but Augustine's echo is clearly audible in Peter's remarks (notwithstanding the fact that Peter's serialization of events and graces carries Augustine's exegesis of the same psalm farther than the African bishop would have wished). This is to say that Peter has not treated altogether unfairly the apostle's straightforward assurance of a relationship between divine and human spirits. His many graces did not annihilate the human spirit. His strategy rather creates the impression that human volition and effort are cradled by grace. For Peter, as for Augustine, Anselm, and Bernard, saving acts are performed according to superior causes, *non secundum naturam* but not *contra naturam*, and not without human will's collaboration.[40]

Among the graces invoked by Peter, perhaps *gratia inhabitans* had the most interesting career in later theology. On Augustine's authority, this grace was taken as the presence or indwelling of the Holy Spirit. Peter, further borrowing from Augustine, identified the indwelling with *caritas*. Some theologians, however, were skeptical about the first equation, and objected that *gratia inhabitans* referred to gifts of the Spirit but not to the Spirit itself. Variations of this perspective slowly came to eclipse the strict identifications of *gratia inhabitans* with the Holy Spirit

---

[40]See Landgraf, *Dogmengeschichte der Frühscholastik* 1.1:141-44. Schupp (*Die Gnadenlehre des Petrus*, p. 40) minimized the importance of Peter's various enumerations and classifications of graces, but the lesson of Peter's many graces is not to be learned exclusively in the comparison between Peter's codifications and those of more systematic thinkers. Compare, for example, *Commentarium in psalmos*, PL 191: 241C-246B with Augustine's *Enarratio in psalmum XXII*, PL 36: 182. Peter devised the serialization of events and graces, but Augustine furnished the general theme.

and both with love.[41] But Peter insisted that love was the mode of the Holy Spirit's presence and the essence of its communication (*"Spiritus testimonium reddit spiritui nostro"*).[42] Love inspired the soul and conformed it to the highest good. The *Sentences* retained the popular notion that *caritas* was a special virtue or habit, but Peter also argued that it was the Spirit's presence that afforded the virtue its special status. More important, he urged that *caritas*, being the Holy Spirit and therefore unlike other gifts of the Holy Spirit, did not require a mediating virtue but could testify (*"reddit testimonium"*) and act directly with and through the Christian's love of God and neighbor.[43]

Peter Lombard's equations are welcome proof that Augustine's synergism had a vital and creative influence on the new shapes assumed by the notion of collaboration. For his part, Peter set forth the connections between spiritual renewal and personal righteousness in a preliminary way in his exegetical works.[44] The *Sentences* then developed the twin ideas that righteousness was the joint work of divine and human wills and that the divine Spirit was present in human love. This, however, placed Peter in a vulnerable position. If the Holy Spirit actually inhered in human righteousness and acted directly without a mediating habit, righteousness could not be said either to increase or to be lost without making the Holy Spirit susceptible to change. Human powers of evil might even extinguish the Spirit as they often extinguish love. Peter indefatigably

---

[41]This is not to say that Peter's influence on this point is undemonstrable. See, for example, *Disputationes Symonis Tornacensis*, ed. Joseph Warichez (Louvain, 1932) d.64.q.2-3 (pp. 178-79). Generally, however, attention was concentrated on the Aristotelian requirement that a mediating form or habit receive and regulate divine action in man, the very notion that Peter confuted. See, inter alia, Johann Auer, *Die Entwicklung der Gnadenlehre in der Hochscholastik*, vol. 2 (Freiburg, 1951); R. P. Réné-Charles Dhont, *Le Problème de la préparation a la grâce* (Paris, 1946); Henri Bouillard, *Conversion et grace chez S. Thomas d'Aquin* (Paris, 1944); Bernard Lonergan, *Grace and Freedom*, ed. J. Patout Burns (New York, 1971); and, with special reference to later scholastic *Habituslehren*, Karl Holl, *"Die justitia dei* in der vorlutherischen Bibelauslegung des Abendlandes," in *Gesammelte Aufsätze zur Kirchengeschichte*, vol. 3 (Darmstadt, 1965), pp. 181-88.

[42]*Libri sententiarum* 1.d.17.2.

[43]Ibid., 1.d.1.3 and d.17.6.

[44]See especially *Collectanea in epist. D. Pauli*, PL 192: 205C-D.

defended his equation against this implication. He insisted that growth in righteousness implied only increased measures of the same Spirit and not the presence of a mutable and therefore counterfeit spirit, and that incipient *caritas* but not perfect love could be lost.[45] But equally industrious theologians were convinced that Peter was mistaken on this point. Aristotle enabled them to register their opposition in fresh and innovative ways, but they were ways that soon obscured the mystical and even the voluntarist elements of Augustine's soteriology.

From Speculative to Experiential Theology, An Interlude

The unmediated presence of the Holy Spirit in human righteousness presumed the infinite bounty of divine grace. Collaboration with God's spirit converted personal moral choices to effects of grace, too numerous and diverse for handy classification. The thirteenth century, however, was unreceptive to ambiguity. The notion that the Spirit must act through mediating habits gained clear ascendancy, as did the conviction that the infinite effects of grace should be "reduced to a definite number of kinds" ("*omnes reducuntur ad aliqua determinata in specie*").[46] Both ideas were products of an Aristotelian temperament most commonly associated with the mature Thomas Aquinas but prevalent throughout the later thirteenth century and lasting well beyond it. The speculative content of Augustinian soteriology achieved greater stature than the voluntarist and mystical elements, which only later were reputed as

---

[45]*Libri sententiarum* 1.d.17.5: "Utrum concedendum sit quod Spiritus Sanctus augeatur in homine et magis vel minus habeatur vel detur. Hic quaeritur, si caritas Spiritus Sanctus est, cum ipsa augeatur et minuatur in homine, et magis et minus per divisa tempora habeatur, utrum concedendum sit quod Spiritus Sanctus augeatur vel minuatur in homine, et magis vel minus habeatur. Si enim in homine augeatur et magis vel minus datur et habetur, mutabilis esse videtur; Deus autem omnino immutabilis est; videtur ergo quod vel Spiritus Sanctus non sit caritas vel caritas non augeatur vel minuatur in homine. . . . His ita respondemus, dicentes quod Spiritus Sanctus sive caritas penitus immutabilis est, nec in se augetur vel minuitur, nec in se recipit magis vel minus, sed in homine vel potius homini augetur et minuitur, et magis vel minus datur vel habetur: sicut Deus dicitur magnificari et exaltari in nobis, qui tamen in se nec magnificatur nec exaltatur." On the concept of growth in righteousness in Peter's exegetical works as well as in the *Sentences*, see Schupp, *Die Gnadenlehre des Petrus*, pp. 266-75.

[46]*Summa theologiae* 1a, 2ae.11.3. Also see Lonergan, *Grace and Freedom*, pp. 99-101.

important for the concrete concern with the Christian life and the reform of the church.[47]

The first of several steps toward this later development was taken at the end of the thirteenth century; for even as Aristotle was warmly welcomed and as his prestige increased, suspicion arose that systems incorporating both the Stagarite's impressive witness for natural reason and the traditional defenses of the supernatural truths of faith could do justice to neither. Aquinas, himself equally at home with the languages of the Greek councils and the Greek philosophers, should have been above suspicion, but his followers were soon *defensores.*[48] Their first task was to clear their master of charges that he was an Averroist. Notwithstanding their immediate successes, the spirit that characterized the accusations was the spirit of the coming age. Responsible for the thirteenth-century Parisian condemnations of Averroism, that spirit also reached far into the next centuries and hammered a wedge between philosophy and theology. Fourteenth-century scholars, trying to reclaim "a purer interpretation of Aristotle" than the one offered by speculative theologians, discovered that Aristotle himself resisted his persistent theological rehabilitation. The Thomist system, in many of its particulars, appeared to them as a clever but ultimately clumsy conspiracy to deprive Aristotle and Augustine of their rightful sovereignties in philosophy and theology respectively. Invariably Thomism found *defensores* in successive generations, but in the fourteenth century the authority of philosophy in theology came to be rivaled by the authority of *experientia.*[49]

---

[47]Auer, *Die Entwicklung der Gnadenlehre,* 2:202-19, 250-55.

[48]Consult James A. Weisheipl, *Friar Thomas D'Aquino: His Life, Thought, and Work* (New York, 1974), p. 164.

[49]See Heiko A. Oberman, "Fourteenth-Century Religious Thought: A Premature Profile," *Speculum* 53 (1978): 80-93. On Aquinas's voluntarism and spirituality and on the somewhat troublesome relationship contracted between Aristotle (spirit known in the act of an external particular object) and Augustine (Spirit known in human faculties as an act of possession), see Klaus Riesenhuber, *Die Transzendenz der Freiheit zum Guten* (Munich, 1971), pp. 292-95. Although the credibility of *experientia* increased in the fourteenth century, especially among the now celebrated mystics, persons who remained most faithful to Augustine's synergism appealed, in customary scholastic fashion, to passages accumulated from supportive texts and not to the personal experience and Pauline suggestions of God's collaboration in righteousness. On Gregory of Rimini, see

However lightly the present study touches upon this medieval shift from speculative, academic theology to experiential theology and to a revitalized Augustinian or voluntarist mysticism, the contribution of Jean Gerson should not be overlooked. Gerson's career as university chancellor (Paris) and conciliarist marks one point at which the reappraisal of speculative theology turned for more than a passing glance at problems of personal regeneration and church reform.[50] He complained at the end of the fourteenth century that his colleagues indulged in vain and narrow curiosities and that they had drifted far from the sources for theology in religious life. Gerson suggested that a theologian was shaped by profound experiential knowledge of divine law, a knowledge that should be applied to reform ecclesiastical law and discipline.[51] But the current wisdom directed scholars elsewhere and left unchecked abuses of ecclesiastical privilege. Academicians, according to Gerson, still inverted the proper order of the soul's powers, wrongly assigning to intellect and speculation the place reserved for the highest affective power and great passion of the soul, *synderesis*.[52] Prelates meanwhile had lost command of scriptural

Eduard Stakemeier, *Der Kampf um Augustin auf dem Tridentum* (Paderborn, 1937), pp. 22-32; and on Thomas Bradwardine, Archbishop of Canterbury for the final thirty-eight days of his life (1349), and the most penetrating of the fourteenth-century controversialists, see Heiko A. Oberman, *Archbishop Thomas Bradwardine, A Fourteenth-Century Augustinian* (Utrecht, 1958). Also note, however, the view that Bradwardine "depresses man even more than . . . Saint Augustine" and the general interpretation of "ruthless grace" in Bradwardine's *De causa dei* argued by Gordon Leff, *Bradwardine and the Pelagians* (Cambridge, 1957). Careful reading of *De causa dei* 3:1-2 (London, 1618) vindicates Oberman's more balanced reading of Bradwardine's Augustinian soteriology. See pp. 637-39 and note "Actus liberi voluntatis sint nobilissimi omnium" and "Si quis autem voluerit dicere, quod Deus potest necessitare hominem ad actum voluntatis, sed hoc facto, non erit hujusmodi actus liber, potest sibi faciliter contradicti."

[50]Review Steven E. Ozment, "The University and the Church: Patterns of Reform in Jean Gerson," *Mediaevalia et humanistica*, n.s., 1 (1970): 111-26; André Combes, *La Théologie mystique de Gerson*, 2 vols. (Rome, 1963-1964); and Louis B. Pascoe, *Jean Gerson: Principles of Church Reform* (Leiden, 1973).

[51]"De vita spirituali animae," *Lectio* 4, in Gerson's *Oeuvres complètes*, ed. Palemon Glorieux (Tournai, 1962).

[52]"Ad Deum vadit," ibid. 5 (1963): 7-8: "Pes amoris in via hac Dei saepe intrat ubi cognitionis pes foris stat; quamvis itaque ambulando in via Dei modo praetacto dum pede fidei praeposito subsequitur pes dilectionis, trahi possit consequenter pes cognitionis ad ulteriora, propinquiori luce cognoscenda, eundo sic pede post pedem; attamen pes amoris

resources for inspiring the Christian life. Unreliable methods of positive and punitive law came to dominate church order and they gave the theologian no significant responsibility for the cure of the church's ills and for the restoration of its pastoral mission. Gerson simply seized that responsibility, although much of his later energy was spent on ill-fated conciliar attempts at institutional reorganization. He died in 1429, some forty years before the birth of one who would again dare to suggest connections between the reform of theology and the reform of church life.

Augustine, Colet, and Erasmus

John Colet struck Erasmus of Rotterdam as the sponsor, though presumably not the originator, of a truly Christian renaissance.[53] The breathless speculations of contemporary theologies—breathless in that they were spectacularly complex and, from Erasmus's point of view, devoid of life—must have appeared awkward and pallid next to the very humanity of Colet's theology. Colet bridged the gap between doctrine and life farther downstream from Gerson's effort and with significantly different design. Gerson spoke of the union and collaboration of divine

---

dexter sublimius semper extendi potest pro hac vis quam sinister. Haec est theologia mystica, id est occulta. Haec scientia propria catholicorum, hoc manna absconditum, hic calculus in quo est nomen novum quod nemo novit nisi qui accipit." For Aquinas, however, *synderesis* was an intellectual habit. Gerson did not closely follow Thomas, but neither did he propose the divorce of *synderesis* and reason ("*Nec tamen excluditur synderesis rationisque consensus*"). Sacred truths grasped by *synderesis* were, as Combes observed (2:241-43), shared with reason, thus advancing the spiritual life.

[53]*Opus epistolarum Des. Erasmi Roterodami*, ed. P. S. Allen, H. M. Allen, and H. W. Garrod, 12 vols. (Oxford, 1906-1958) 4: 94, lines 43-46. Written under the influence of Frederic Seebohm's magisterial but all too partisan *The Oxford Reformers* (3rd ed. London: Longmans, Green, 1887), Joseph Lupton's biography is still the most authoritative: *A Life of Dean Colet*, 2nd ed. (London, 1909). Reconstruction of Colet's life, however, requires some guesswork. His birthdate is uncertain. Generally he is assumed to have been educated at Oxford, but records for the years of his probable matriculation and attendance have been lost. W. Robert Godfrey marshaled considerable yet not conclusive evidence for his opinion that Colet was schooled along the Cam: "John Colet of Cambridge," *Archiv für Reformationsgeschichte* 65 (1974): 6-18. Colet's continental itinerary (1493-1496/7), the chronology of his lectures and occasional treatises, and the date of his move from Oxford lectern to London pulpit as Dean of St. Paul's Cathedral (1504 or 1505) similarly cannot be established beyond question.

and human wills in terms of the person's ecstatic love of God, a voluntarist mysticism without a correspondent moral theology.[54] Colet understood the return of God's love through love of neighbor as the highest expression of God's collaboration with man. He lectured that this understanding was fundamental to Pauline spirituality and to church reform,[55] and this idea immediately captivated his visitor from the continent. When they first met in 1499, John Colet had been lecturing at Oxford on the Pauline epistles for three years and Erasmus for several years longer had been studying at Paris where the university's faculty was dominated by Scotists. The two shared a dislike of scholasticism's elaborate speculations and classifications, although Colet's disapprobation included Aquinas while Erasmus's did not.[56] Erasmus clearly perceived that his host's Oxford lectures presented something of an alternative to speculative theology, but that alternative has not yet been reconstructed fully and catalogued as a chapter in the Augustinian voluntarist tradition. Erasmus himself has been largely to blame for this failure.

First Erasmus recklessly employed encomiastic and misleading language to celebrate his friend's talents. To students of Erasmus's correspondence this will seem a familiar and forgivable fault, and the fact that Erasmus returned from Oxford with a demonstrable excitement about St.

---

[54] See Pascoe, *Jean Gerson*, p. 206; but also Combes, *La Théologie mystique*, 2:506-8 on Gerson's opposition to "préquiétisme."

[55] Erasmus believed that Colet lectured on all the epistles (Allen 4: 515, line 282). The notes that survive have been edited and translated by Joseph H. Lupton (*Epistolae B. Pauli ad Romanos expositio, Enarratio in epsitolam B. Pauli ad Romanos, Enarratio in epistolam primam S. Pauli ad Corinthios*, and *De corpore Christi mystico*, which probably constitutes a fragment of a separate selection of lectures). The lectures along with abstracts of the Pseudo-Dionysius's *Hierarchies*, interpretations of Genesis, and a treatise on the sacraments were originally printed in five volumes in London between 1867 and 1876, and they have been reprinted in four volumes by Gregg International Press (Farnborough, United Kingdom and Ridgewood, New Jersey, 1965-1966). All translations that follow are mine, but references to Lupton's translations are included when discrepancies suggest different understandings of Colet's meaning.

[56] Allen, *Opus epistolarum*, 4:520, lines 424-34. Consult also Paul Mestwerdt, *Die Anfänge des Erasmus: Humanismus und "Devotio Moderna"* (Leipzig, 1917), pp. 317, 332-34; and Edward L. Surtz, Jr. "Oxford Reformers and Scholasticism," *Studies in Philology* 47 (1950): 547-56. But also note the eccentric, albeit not entirely unconvincing approach to Erasmus's viewpoint in Christian Dolfen's *Die Stellung des Erasmus von Rotterdam zur scholastischen Methode* (Osnabrück, 1936).

Paul should speak eloquently about Colet's real influence and interests.[57] Erasmus's pairing of Colet and Plato, however, laid foundations for exhaustive but essentially one-sided studies of Colet's Neoplatonism.[58] "The key to Colet's entire body of thought," Leland Miles intoned, "is the fact that it is built around four parallel adaptations of Plotinian emana-tion." Scratch Colet's restoration of the Pauline doctrine of justification, and the countenance of Marsilio Ficino glares back at you.[59] Sears Jayne in his study of Colet's *"Marginalia"* in the All Souls College manuscript of Ficino's *Epistolae* has done incalculable service to Colet scholarship by reasserting Colet's theological and expressly Pauline preoccupation with the work of the great Florentine humanist.[60] Still, much damage has been

---

[57]Erasmus landed on the continent with only his recollections of pleasant learned conversations with his Oxford friend, but he had other friends send him a parcel stuffed with an overcoat, a copy of Augustine's *Enchiridion*, and copies of St. Paul's letters (Allen, *Opus epistolarum*, 1:286-87, lines 19-25; 1:315, lines 56-61; and 1:323, lines 119-22). He may never have received the parcel; nevertheless he was soon absorbed in his own first commentaries on the Pauline correspondence, now lost, and he reported completion of four volumes (Allen, *Opus epistolarum*, 1:404, lines 31-34). He was still at work on the commentary when he was solicited for a manual of practical theology, which was written as the *Enchiridion militis Christianae* (*Enchiridion*, p. 135, lines 33-35). When Erasmus announced ten years later that he might again take up his work on the letters of St. Paul, he wrote to Colet from Cambridge, "perhaps I shall dare to approach *your* Paul (*"Paulum tuum"*). See Allen, *Opus epistolarum*, 1:466, lines 16-20; and *infra*, chapter 5.

[58]Allen, *Opus epistolarum*, 1:273, line 21: "Coletum meum cum audio, Platonem ipsum mihi videor audire."

[59]See Leland Miles, *John Colet and The Platonic Tradition* (LaSalle, Illinois, 1961), pp. 135 and 167. Also review Ernest William Hunt, *Dean Colet and His Theology* (London, 1956), pp. 103-30; and Patrick Bernard O'Kelly, "John Colet's *Enarratio in primam S. Pauli epistolam ad Corinthios*. A New Edition of the Text with Translation, Notes, and Introduction" (Ph.D. Dissertation, Harvard University, 1960), pp. 99, 103-105, 110. The latter concludes (pp. 121-22) that "Colet does not by any means altogether satisfy the mind as to the relationship between normative principles of conduct with regard to sensible phenomena and a mysticism of being and becoming in intelligible order of existence"—a point that the pages following here will contest vigorously. Miles, Hunt, and O'Kelly represent the advanced stages of an interpretation of Colet's neoplatonism pioneered by Kurt Schroeder and Friedrich Dannenberg. See Schroeder's *Platonismus in der englischen Renaissance vor und bei Thomas Eliot* (Berlin, 1920) and Dannenberg's *Das Erbe Platons in England bis zur Bildung Lylys* (Berlin, 1932).

[60]Sears Jayne, *John Colet and Marsilio Ficino* (London, 1963), pp. 47, 51-52, 54, 67-68. (Arrangement of the *Marginalia* [pp. 84-132] makes it convenient to place them with any

done; and Jayne's corrective, though it goes a long way, goes only part of the way. It establishes beyond doubt that Colet never met Ficino, notwithstanding his visit to Florence before he returned to England and began his Oxford lectures.[61] Moreover, Colet's applications of Ficino's *Theologia Platonica* to biblical exegesis in the lectures were infrequent and were more a matter of opportunism than a strategy derived from thoughtful integration of Plato and Paul. Although nearly twenty years have passed since Jayne suggested that Colet's thought might best be explored as an extension of Augustine's voluntarism, no scholar has taken up the task.[62] The influence of Erasmus's overstatement has been qualified, but the unfortunate impact of another of the great humanist's unreliable remarks has not yet been eliminated.

Erasmus's short and commendatory biography of Colet was addressed to Justus Jonas in 1521. The author had much to say about his subject's activities and personal interests; but when the biography, which was accompanied by an equally commendatory life of Jean Vitrier, is read with an eye for the interest of the intended reader, the report takes on a distinctly polemical character. Erasmus noted that Colet was more unfavorably disposed (*"iniquior"*) toward Augustine than toward any other church father.[63] And the fact that Colet explicitly cited the greatest of Latin theologians only five times in the lectures that survive tempts one to take for granted the accuracy of Erasmus's account, until it is remembered that Colet very seldom expressed his debts and that the few direct references to Augustine were deferential and more numerous than references to any other church father or theologian, save St. Paul and the pseudo-Dionysius.[64] The several instances where Colet turned to Augustine might easily have been missed by Erasmus, whose visit to Oxford

---

copy of the 1495 *Epistolae*.) Jayne's chronology of Colet's lectures is plausible. There is reason, however, to suspect his dating of the abstracts of the Pseudo-Dionysius's *Hierarchies* and the *De sacramentis ecclesiae* (pp. 29-31, 34). See my "The Soteriological Center of the Thought of John Colet" (Ph.D. Dissertation, University of Chicago, 1975), p. 9, note 2.

[61]Jayne, *John Colet*, pp. 18-21.

[62]Ibid., p. 75.

[63]Allen, *Opus epistolarum*, 4:515, line 273.

[64]EER-a, pp. 230-31, 245, 253; and EER-b, pp. 160, 180.

lasted only a few months. The biographer might also be excused for overlooking the connection between Colet's voluntarist mysticism and that present in Augustine's soteriology, for Colet himself may have remained as unaware as the generations of Colet scholars of the full implications of his own concepts of righteousness and reform. But Erasmus's *"iniquior"* is unpardonable. Nothing currently known supports the suggestion of Colet's intense disapproval. Erasmus was simply slanting the profile of his deceased friend in order to urge upon his correspondent Jonas a model of reform dramatically different from the one provoked by the then recent events in Saxony. Jonas, a young humanist contemplating Lutheran partisanship, would have been sensitive to the observation that one tremendously admirable reformer discredited Augustine, the very theologian lionized by the reformation that appealed to him.[65] If Erasmus's remark is read as part of the overall strategy of his letter and biography, namely, to win Jonas away from Luther, it deters no one from taking seriously the affinities between Colet and Augustine.

What follows here is an elaborate contradiction of Erasmus's *"iniquior."* Colet's attitude toward Augustine does not belong among the passions and hatreds generated by religious controversy during that tumultuous age, but the similarities between their thinking on grace, human will, and righteousness do belong in the history of Christian thought and in the search for the roots of sixteenth-century Catholic reform. The one scholar who best recognized the specious character of parts of Erasmus's biography elected to emphasize the close relationship alleged between the pessimistic anthropologies of Colet and Augustine. Eugene Rice harvested a crop of quotations from the Oxford lectures that presents Colet as "an ascetic . . . who systematically destroys the natural in order to preserve the divine omnipotence and goodness from any hint of mockery or derogation."[66] From what has been said here, in the first two

---

[65]See Heinz Holeczek, "Die Haltung des Erasmus zu Luther nach dem Scheitern seiner Vermittlungspolitik 1520/1," *Archiv für Reformationsgeschichte* 64 (1973): 91-92, 108-9.

[66]Eugene F. Rice, Jr., "John Colet and the Annihilation of the Natural," *Harvard Theological Review* 45 (1952): 147-48. On the "austere vision of life" in English humanism, see Piero Rebora, "Aspetti dell'Umanesimo in Inghilterra," *La Rinascita* 2 (1939): 386; and on humanism and asceticism, see Francis Hermans, *Histoire doctrinale de*

chapters, it should be obvious that, if this were true, it would open a chasm between Colet and Augustine rather than close the one created by Erasmus's remark. But it remains to return Rice's harvest to the fields whence it came and to inspect Colet's lectures for the understandings of righteousness and reform that will make intelligible his relation to the Augustinian soteriological tradition and his influence upon Erasmus and upon the cause of Catholic reform.

---

l'humanisme Chrétien, 4 vols. (Paris, 1948) 4: 111-29. For a more recent treatment of Colet's antipathies, consult H. C. Porter, "The Gloomy Dean and the Law: John Colet 1466-1519," *Essays in Modern English Church History in Memory of Norman Sykes*, ed. G. V. Bennett and J. D. Walsh (New York, 1966), pp. 18-34, but also note the profile of Colet's "asceticism" and pre-Elizabethan "puritanism" that can be assembled from H. Maynard Smith's *Prereformation England* (London, 1938). All the above must be read in the light of Catherine A. L. Jarrott's recent and expertly argued dissent ("To Colet the world of the Christian is not a vale of tears but a grace-filled, love-filled existence of endless opportunity for spiritual growth"), "Erasmus's Annotations and Colet's Commentaries on Paul: A Comparison of Some Theological Themes," *Essays on the Works of Erasmus*, ed. Richard L. De Molen (New Haven, 1978), p. 131.

3　　*John Colet: In Propagatione Justitiae*

Faith, Hope, and Works of Righteousness

In John Colet's second set of lectures on St. Paul's letter to the Romans, the short discussion of the fourth chapter is completely given over to an examination of Abraham's righteousness. The patriarch's faith was considered much more effective in achieving his special place in divine favor than were the observances of his coreligionists. According to Colet, Abraham received God's promise more in faith than in circumcision; and this was precisely what the apostle desired to stress. St. Paul separated justification and the dispensation of God's grace from any merit that might accrue to humankind or even to God's elect for their scrupulous performances of ceremonies and their observances of ritual restrictions. Colet's reading of St. Paul's epistle convinced him that Abraham's faith, both as a gift from God and as a human response to divine generosity, was irrefragable assurance of God's love.[1]

When Colet spoke here of Abraham's faith, he was thinking of the patriarch's confidence in God (*"confidit Deo"*); but in one of his earliest lectures on Romans, he preferred to define faith as simple assent to what was preached and taught about Christ.[2] (Only if these earliest remarks are

---

[1]EER-b, pp. 140-41. Also note EER-a, p. 269 and EER-b, p. 182.
[2]EER-a, pp. 230-34.

taken as constitutive of Colet's fully formed position can the late medieval introduction of and emphasis upon the fiducial aspect of faith be pushed beyond Colet and attributed to Erasmus and later evangelical humanists.[3]) But as Colet continued his commentaries on the Pauline epistles, he appears to have forgotten his early definition. He keenly sensed that "men of little faith are in jeopardy" (*homines modicae fidei periclitantur*), and this compelled him to reopen the investigation and to discriminate between the several ways in which scripture uses *"fides."* He decided that the meaning intended *"multo frequentissime"* was fiduciality and not credulity. In all, save the first, reflections upon the nature and centrality of faith, Colet scaled down the importance of discreet *credenda*. Increasing weight was given to *"fiducia et spes in potentia Dei"* as a personal response to God's grace and God's promises of salvation.[4]

Following St. Paul, Colet called attention to the role of grace in the achievement of Abraham's confidence.

> God gives himself through his grace to persons who believe and trust in him and who have been drawn by him from infidelity to faith. Thus they trust only in God and they believe that they can be justified in no other way than by divine grace. The law, as the object of the Jews' hopes, defines sin, prescribes limits, threatens transgressors. But the law does not remove the fault, release man from his constraints, cherish and sustain him graciously. Divine grace does all this firmly but gently so that one is able to trust only in God. This grace touched, attracted, and justified Abraham; and it promised him that an inestimable number of persons would be equally and similarly justified.[5]

---

[3]Cf. Lowell C. Green, "The Influence of Erasmus upon Melanchthon, Luther, and the Formula of Concord in the Doctrine of Justification," *Church History* 43 (1974): 188.

[4]See, for example, EEC, pp. 237-38.

[5]EER-b, p. 140: "Qui ex sua gratia se impartit credentibus sibi et confidentibus, quos idem ipse exemit et abstraxit ab infidelitate ad fidem, ut ei soli confidant, credantque plane nulla se alia ratione nisi divina gratia justificari posse. Quoniam lex, in qua speraverunt Judei, peccatum indicat, terminos praescribit, transgressoribus minitatur; non tollit quidem delictum, non trahit hominem ab augustiis, non gratiose fovet et sustinet. Quod quidem divina gratia et fortiter et suaviter facit, ut soli Deo possit confidere. Quae gratia attigit et attraxit et justificavit Abraam, promisitque illi quamplurimos, et ad numerum etiam stellarum, pariter ac similiter homines justificatos fore."

Colet concluded several pages later that "all hope for salvation must be placed in faith so that men trust thereafter only in God."[6]

Hope appears to be a lower level of fiduciality. Aquinas also acknowledged that hope was the *"introitus fidei,"* but by this he meant that hope furnished the *rei creditae* and he argued that hope itself was founded upon the enlightenment of faith. Faith furnished the *rei speratae,* the promises that inspired hope. In the *Summa theologiae* the virtue of hope presupposed faith and, to some extent, the meritorious works that followed from faith, both of which saved the believer from groundless and misdirected aspirations.[7] Colet, however, truly believed that "hope is the beginning of the human odyssey to God."

> Faith, hope, and charity are simultaneously infused into the soul by that one beautiful spirit of God. But if nothing prohibits a possible order in instantaneous occurrences and an establishment of first, second, and third, then surely reason shows that faith precedes charity and hope precedes faith, inasmuch as hope consists of unity, faith of light, and charity of zeal. If the order of things requires that something must first be united before illumined and illumined before set ablaze with zeal, then it is necessary that hope which is a certain unity and stability of the spirit holds first place.[8]

As unity and stability, hope is neither easily cultivated nor effortlessly sustained. Hope demands, according to Colet, the surrender of self-

---

[6]EER-b, p. 158: "[O]stendit [Paulus] spem salutis omnem esse positam in fide, ut homines soli Deo confidant."

[7]*Summa theologiae* 1a 2ae, 65, 4; 2a 2ae, 17, 1 and 7.

[8]EER-b, pp. 182-83: "Quae spes initium est humanae profectionis in Deum, quae est collectio animae et counitio ac contractio in Deum ut illuminetur et incendatur. . . . Sunt quidem haec tria, fides spes et charitas, a Dei spiritu uno bono et pulchro simul eodem momento in animam infusa. Verumtamen, si nihil prohibeat quin in momentaniis ordo excogitari possit, et primum, secundum et tertium statuere, profecto ratio exposit ut fides charitati, spes fidei antecedat. Quandoquidem spes unitione, fides lumine, charitas ardore consistit. Quod si rerum ordo exigit ut prius quodque sit unione quam luceat, prius luceat quam ardeat, profecto tum necesse sit, ut primum locum teneat spes, quae est quaedam unitio et stabilitas animi; secundum fides, quae illustratio mentis et Dei cognitio; tertium et ultimum charitas, qui amor est cogniti Dei et desiderium." Colet's earliest lectures (EER-a, pp. 242, 248) establish this order, and later lectures generally maintain it. See, for example, EEC, pp. 227-28, 245-46, 256-58. But also note the few exceptions, EEC, pp. 206, 283.

reliance in the light of the central proclamation of the Pauline epistles: the grace of Jesus Christ has overcome the power of sin. One must acknowledge the folly of self-trust, "recognize one's errors, deplore one's sins, beg for grace, and patiently, purely, and innocently offer oneself to God so that one may be touched, moved, and affected by grace . . . and be reformed into a new man."[9] Elsewhere Colet spoke of this as purification and purgation, and he implied throughout that human effort was necessary to relinquish self-reliance and to repose complete trust in God: "Seeking precedes adoption, self-management precedes soundness, washing and cleansing precede advance." Hope gathers all affections and concentrates them upon God, and faith seals the confidence inspired by hope with the certainty that what is hoped for has indeed been promised and vouchsafed by God.[10]

In hope, as in faith, that is, as confidence in God is increasingly established, grace works "firmly but gently." The possibility of fiduciality is given with the infusion of the spirit, but the believer's advances in "self-management" and purgation are accomplished by grace and human will working cooperatively. The interpenetration of grace and will in Colet's soteriology matches the convergence of the righteousness of faith with the righteousness of works advocated in Colet's lectures. Faith discloses the pathways to the heavenly city and also permits the believer a glimpse of the goal, a life of blessedness. Armed with faith, the believer is invincible against the powers of darkness; but faith in Christ's righteous-

---

[9]EER-b, p. 166: "[A]gnoscat errores, deploret peccata, imploret gratiam, offeratque se patientem, purum et simplicem Deo ut a simplici et puro divino radio gratiaque attingi, agitari, affici, et in novum hominem, spiritualem videlicet et divinum, reformari possit." Also consult EER-a, pp. 251, 276-77.

[10]SAC, p. 86: "[P]rocuratio [antecedit] adoptionem, et curatio sanitatem, et lotio ac tersio nitorem." Colet was generally reluctant to speak about hope as *praeparatio* for grace. One of Marsilio Ficino's "*Epistolae*" described a pattern of ascent from civic to divine virtues, assuring readers that every preparation commands its fulfillment. Colet was not persuaded. He reduced Ficino's pattern to a few notations ("*expiatio,*" "*purgatio,*" "*informatio*") and avoided Ficino's formula with respect to preparation. See Ficino's *Opera omnia*, 10 volumes (Basel, 1576; reprinted in Turin, 1959) 1:618-19 and MARG, 14, p. 94. Often, however, Colet associated hope with "*purgatio*" and implied that cleansing and focusing one's affections constituted a preliminary, if not, in the strict sense, preparatory, righteousness. See EER-b, pp. 175-79; PSD, pp. 169-70, 191-93, 207-208, 240; and SAC, p. 77.

ness is insufficient without the performance of righteous works that reflect the object of faith in the lives of the faithful.[11]

Colet commended the life of righteousness as the sure antidote against self-reliance and the legalism inherited from the Jews. In this sense, both faith and works collaborate against the tendencies toward self-reliance that so annoyed St. Paul. Commenting on Romans 2:6, "he will render to every man according to his works," Colet began his second set of lectures on that epistle with the kind of assertion that dominated his reflections on personal salvation and church reform.

> God is no selector and acceptor of persons. He does not regard Jews more graciously than he regards other peoples (as the Jews themselves have thought) because the law had been a unique gift to them. Rather he considers and praises the deeds of those from every nation. . . . The status and praise of a man depend totally on action. Whoever performs well and justly even without the law is considered by God to have lived well according to the law.[12]

Righteous works were so important to Colet that, years later, in his *De sacramentis ecclesiae*, he instructed catechists in no uncertain terms to emphasize *satisfactio operis* in penance. "Satisfaction" must not only compensate for previous wrongdoing but must also tip the scales decisively in favor of the righteous life. And, as if to underscore the fact that performance best prosecutes the penitent's case before God, Colet concluded his treatise on the sacraments with a dramatic call for *"recompensatio"* in terms of an active righteousness.

> Compensation ought always to be made with contrary action such that satisfaction in good be made for evil. The contrary conquers its opposite. Avarice ought to be redeemed by liberality and charity, luxury and drunkenness by continence and fasting, neglect of God by diligent prayer. Thus God may have compassion on you for your unrighteousness.[13]

---

[11]EER-b, pp. 205-206.

[12]EER-b, p. 137: "Quoniam non est selector Deus, et acceptator personarum, nec (uti putaverunt Judei) habet eos, ob legem eis datam peculiarem, sibi quam reliquos gentium multo gratiores. Sed in quaque gente ipsa eorum facta et spectat et laudat. . . . Res et laus hominis tota est posita in actione; quam bonam et justam qui exercuerit, etiam si nullam habuerit sibi legem datam, is tamen a Deo censetur recte secundum legem vixisse."

[13]SAC, p. 92: "Recompensatio in contrario semper debet esse; ut pro malo satisfactio fiat in bono, et ut contrarium contrarium vincat. Avaritia redimenda est liberalitate et

Does this call for "recompensatio" suggest that the penitent alone can earn forgiveness (*"ut injustitia tua Deus misereatur tui"*)? A reading of Colet's many remarks about the importance of moral endeavor might lead some, as it has led C. S. Lewis, to reduce Colet to "a declamatory moralist" and to forget the subtleties of his moral theology. Others who would think of him as a solafideist and precursor of Luther are sure to be scandalized by his enthusiastic employment of the "works righteousness" passage in James's epistle (James 2:14-26) in one of his own expositions of Abraham's faith and righteousness. What must not be forgotten, however, is Colet's conviction that only the spirit permitted the very possibility of the penitent's resolve to hope for and believe in deliverance and the power of the Christian to pursue and achieve righteousness. That this corresponds to Augustine's understanding of grace and will remains to be shown. First Colet's notion that all virtue rests in good works (*"Tota vis in actione boni est"*) and his appreciation for the soteriological significance of moral conduct must be elaborated and placed within the context of his own special interest in St. Paul.

Divine Love and the Moral Life

Faith imparts wisdom to the believer, but Colet was absolutely certain that the righteousness of faith was sufficient for salvation only if the faithful perform works of righteousness. "We know in vain," he declared, "if we do not use our knowledge properly to worship God and lawfully to live among men. Wisdom is assessed as true and firm by virtue of the fruit it bears in our actions toward God and men. Vital wisdom makes man humbly worship God, live temperately, and benefit man lovingly."[14] Christians might become trapped in the conceit that doctrine and faith were secure and salvific without pious practices, but, in Colet's judgment, this would display ignorance of St. Paul's warning that without constant use, "the armor of righteousness" speedily rusts.[15]

---

eleemosyna; luxuria et crapula continentia et jejunio; negligentia Dei oratione assidua, ut injustitia tua Deus misereatur tui."

[14]EER-a, p. 203: "Frustra et inaniter cognoscimus, si ex illa cognitione non colamus Deum rite, et legittime cum hominibus vivamus. Censetur vera et solida sapientia ex fructu actionis Deo et hominibus. Viva sapientia facit hominem humiliter colere Deum, et temperanter vivere, et amanter prodesse hominibus."

[15]EER-a, p. 220; EEC, pp. 197-98; PSD, p. 213.

Colet believed that his remarks on the significance of Christian conduct followed the trail from doctrine and faith to the pious life left by the itinerant ministry of St. Paul. Theory was never remote from the practical problems of the early churches in the apostle's correspondence. St. Paul found the churches of Rome and Corinth in a particularly confused state: Gentiles and Jews disputed about the nature of their shared Christianity; Christians were perplexed by problems presented by their relationships with their heathen compatriots and rulers; differences among Christians as to specific customs and practices further complicated the life of the Roman church. Colet understood St. Paul to have recognized that doctrine had to be responsive to these tangled problems, but he also imagined that St. Paul recognized that a cauldron of opinions already heated by debate and disagreement could not have been cooled by the addition of one more doctrine. Colet observed that the apostle soberly reduced his teaching to three universally applicable counsels: patience, humility, and charity. Their practical usefulness was obvious; their soteriological meaning, perhaps less so. Still, Colet observed that he might establish his own doctrine of the Christian life as well as its importance for salvation upon those counsels, and he was convinced that he could proceed without fear of dishonoring St. Paul's intentions.[16]

The apostle's counsel of charity was, as Colet noted, especially timely. The heterogeneity of the Corinthian church was about to turn into a chaos of conflicting views and practices when the apostle drew the lesson that, if one believes Colet, reversed the trends toward disunity and decline in the early churches and virtually saved Christianity from extinction.

> Paul, the wisest of men, knowing that because of [disagreements about] the offerings of idol meats, the Corinthians were not appropriately enough united, knew also that the cause of that malady was lack of charity. Without charity, nothing can be done well. With charity, nothing can go awry. Paul persuades those who seemed to themselves to be quite knowledgeable that their knowledge of God was useless and even dangerous unless they loved God and unless, in that love, the love of neighbor was included.[17]

---

[16]EER-b, pp. 135-36.

[17]EEC, p. 230: "Paulus autem, homo sapientissimus, intelligens propter immolata idolis Corinthios non satis concinne convenire, cum novit morbi causam esse defectum

Knowledgeable church members must then refer their actions to the well-being of the church and, at times, compromise individual standards of right and wrong, so that Christ's love for the church may be reflected in mutual affections that bind churchmen together into a corporate witness of that love.[18]

The structure of Colet's understanding of charity is buttressed by the acknowledgment of the *amor Dei in nobis*. Justification and sanctification amount to the return of that love. Active righteousness extends the *amor Dei* to neighbors and even to enemies, repays God for the free gift of love, and justifies the righteous person who, like St. Paul, has experienced "the extraordinary force of charity."[19] Strictly speaking, God cannot be said to receive anything. By giving love, however, the believer likens him or herself to the angels who themselves resemble God, confirming divinity more in giving than in receiving love. Colet's commentary on the pseudo-Dionysian *Hierarchies* reiterated the argument sketched in his lectures. "He who does not re-present whatever is impressed upon him cruelly obliterates that 'image.' Insofar as we are all marked by one image, we have received the imprint of one king as if we were his coins, so that we might reflect the One upon whom all depends."[20] The proper work of the

---

charitatis; sine qua nihil recte, cum qua etiam nihil oblique fieri potest; persuadet hic illis, qui sibi sapientiores videbantur, scientiam eorum unius Dei inutilem esse et periculosam, nisi simul eundem diligunt; in quo proximi dilectio continetur."

[18]EER-b, pp. 193, 204.

[19]EER-b, p. 155: "De charitate vere illa a qua nulla se ratione dimoveri posse Paulus dixit, hoc est deinde quod dicamus; quod scilicet charitas et amor idem est; quodque amor Dei in nobis ex amore erga nos Dei excitatur, et ab amante nos Deo in nobis gignitur. Hinc illud Joannis in epistola: 'Charitas ex Deo est': et paulo post addit, 'In hoc est charitas, non quod nos dileximus Deum, sed quod ipse prior dilexit nos.' Itaque, Deo nos amante, ipsum redamamus." Although Colet found in Marsilio Ficino an eloquent spokesman for love's soteriological priority ("fiuntque tandem homines multo meliores amando Deum quam exquirendo"), close attention must be paid to points where Colet parts company from the Florentine Neoplatonist. He agreed with Ficino that all love of wisdom was directly related to piety (MARG, 3, p. 87; Ficino, *Opera omnia*, 1:608). He was relatively uninterested, however, in Ficino's preoccupation in the *Epistolae* with contemplative love. Colet's chief concern was the love that spends itself in active righteousness. See EER-b, pp. 143, 157; and Jayne, pp. 68-70.

[20]PSD, p. 200: "Obliterat enim imaginem nepharie, qui non repraesentat id quatenus percutitur. Siquidem omnes sumus ad unum sigillum signati, et unius regis character, quasi numisma illius, accepimus; ut unum, unde pendeant omnia, referamus."

faithful then is simply the extension of God's love for creation through man's love for his neighbors (in Colet's terms, *"opus . . . ardentissimae charitatis"*), and this is the very essence of active righteousness (*"opus justissimum"*).[21]

It would be difficult to overestimate the fundamental role that charity plays in John Colet's thoughts on redemption. *"Complet et consummat omnia charitas, quae approbatur a Deo"*; charity completes all things that God approves. It is therefore of a higher magnitude (*"coactior"* and *"unitior"*) than is faith, and the premium that Colet placed upon charity as opposed to faith and knowledge indicates the soteriological preeminence of active righteousness that not only resolves institutional conflicts but also advances God's love throughout creation.[22]

Colet thought that St. Paul's prescription of patience and humility had been calculated to produce one of two immediate and favorable political results. Roman authorities might more easily be induced to regard the infant church as harmless, were churchmen to forbear the wrongdoing of their persecutors. Rome might then either neglect the church's existence, or, optimally, protect it from its enemies. St. Paul had not anticipated that the decline of paganism would have left unsolved the problems of the Christian citizen, but Colet realized that evil and aggression were inherent in the very nature of political authority. The fifteenth-century Christian, according to Colet, was victimized by formidable laws and decrees that marked the self-intoxication of authority. The proliferation of legislation and ordinances for exhaustive regulation of the Christian life dramatized the sins of self-assertion and disorder in both secular and ecclesiastical governments. Colet, therefore, returned to the political wisdom of the apostle's counsel.[23] But the greater part of Colet's own counsel of forebearance was the confidence that patience outlasts provocations and ultimately converts provocateurs. Patience itself becomes a *Machtfaktor* insofar as good vanquishes evil; and, as Colet interpreted the apostle's prescription of patience and humility, the axiom *"Nihil est quod vincit malum nisi bonum"* was situated at its center.[24]

[21]SAC, p. 37; EEC, pp. 259-64.

[22]EEC, p. 256.

[23]EER-b, pp. 198-204. Also see EER-a, pp. 258-60, 266, 279-81.

[24]EER-b, pp. 194-97.

Christ's passion forces upon the faithful an inescapable heritage of humility and patience. The incarnation as well presents a consummate demonstration of humility that throws a Christian's self-reliance and self-esteem into painful relief. Incarnation and passion were, according to Colet, free lessons for the Christian life. The Jews thought of Christ's humility as a symptom of his weakness, but the believer knows Christ's patient suffering as a sign of strength and accepts Christ's forbearance as a model of unflinching humility.[25]

Whereas Matthew (27:39-44) reported the abuses heaped upon the suffering savior, St. Paul turned that report into the cornerstone of his soteriology, a *theologia crucis* that made of Christ's humility and patience the very motive-power of the Christian life. Colet inferred that the perceptible moral power in powerlessness certified divine favor. Whoever is considered humble and meek in the eyes of men and must patiently endure their scorn is esteemed virtuous in the eyes of God. Without Christ's example, however, the inference might have remained simply a guess. But Christ's constancy assured patience and humility of their place in moral theology and their importance for soteriology. Hope rivets one's every thought and deed to God; but forbearance—set as it is before neighbor and persecutor—is the dramatic declaration of hope and its expression in active righteousness as well as a confession of the power over theology and over the Christian life exercised by Christ's righteousness.[26]

Concern with the meaning of Christ's incarnation and resurrection stretches across all Colet's commentaries. Christ's incarnation was immediately suggestive for Colet of the bounty and mercy of God. As propitiator, Christ established his dominion over the world when he reconciled to God persons who would otherwise have languished in sin and disorder.[27]

---

[25]EER-b, pp. 178-81, 215-216.

[26]EEC, pp. 167-71, 201.

[27]Colet took some interest in the neoplatonic reconstruction of Christ's "cosmic" ministry and mission. His elaboration of the pseudo-Dionysius's *Hierarchies* affords a glimpse of a nine-fold sublunar order awaiting the condescension (in this context, a better word than "incarnation") of an archetype that would establish perfect symmetry in the terrestrial worlds as God himself had established it in the angelic worlds. See PSD, especially pp. 173-74, 188-89. More commonly, however, Colet sketched the personal impact of Christ's historical mission in less speculative and, one might say, more pastoral terms. See EER-a, pp. 229-30; EER-b, pp. 151-52, 215; and EEC, p. 171.

The most constant feature of Colet's christology, however, is the emphasis placed upon Christ's life as the expression of God's will written in the vernacular of moral achievement.

Colet's earliest lectures put what one might call the moral proposition of his christology into its most compact form: "Look back upon Christ, the most splendid example of living. Re-form yourself to him. Re-present him in your whole life."[28] His second set of lectures on Romans equally stressed the necessity to practice what Christ set forth in his deeds and convictions.[29] The same theme also runs through Colet's commentary on Corinthians:

> The heavenly man Jesus in his own life, as if teaching and speaking plainly, taught men in what manner that celestial perfection might be manifest in humanity. All who wish to be His in reality as well as in name should try to imitate that perfection, to direct their lives toward that common target set before all men, as if shooting for life so that they might achieve the same life by which every life is measured. He will be accounted either to life or to damnation to the extent that he is either closer or more distant on earth to that target.[30]

When, in later life, Colet founded St. Paul's School he declared that the manners of the "good Christian lyff" were as important as the increase of knowledge and the habit of worship, and he solicited from Erasmus *"Carmina scholaria"* that unmistakably identified that "lyff" with the *imago pueri Jesu.*[31]

---

[28]EER-a, p. 227: "Respiciat Christum, praeclarissimum vivendi exemplum; reformet se illi; tota denique vita representet illum. . . ."

[29]EER-b, p. 169.

[30]EEC, pp. 208-209: "Cujusmodi autem profectio illa coelestis in hominibus sit, docuit ipse Jesus homo coelestis sua ipsa vita, quasi loquens expressius et instruens homines. Quam profecto est omnium totis conatibus imitari, qui illius tam re quam nomine haberi volunt, et tanquam ad commune signum, propositum omnibus, illuc dirigere vitam, ut prope quasi sagittantes ad vitam, ipsam vitam lucrentur, qua mensurabuntur omnia. Atque ut quisque hic in terris ad illud signum se habet vel propinquius vel distantius, sic et talis profecto illa et ad damnationem et ad vitam censebitur."

[31]See Colet's *"Statuta Paulinae Scholae,"* in Lupton's *Life of Dean Colet,* pp. 271-84. Also consult Karl Hartfelder, "Das Ideal einer Humanistenschule," *Verhandlungen der Versammlungen deutscher Philologen und Schulmanner* 41 (1892): 166-81; Rudolf

Christ's incarnation and resurrection inform the Christian of what God has done for him. The moral proposition of Colet's christology informs the Christian of what he must do for himself. The *pro nobis* of the cross did not waive the exacting claims upon believers' lives that form, according to Colet, Christ's special legacy. The believer cannot station himself in Christ's righteousness without imitating Christ's life, for all that has been promised and that sustains hope and faith is only part of the kerygma.

> Some of what Christ proclaimed ought to be done in this life; some ought to be anticipated for the next life. What ought to be done here is the striving from love of the good after the upright, pious, and just way of life that Christ, as Exemplar, showed us in Himself. What ought to be anticipated is that 'eternal weight of glory' that is sublime and above all else and that the imitation of Christ works in us as we contemplate that which we do not yet see. With the desire of so great and so beatific a reward, we ought to follow the One who went before us. That is, in the exhausting course set by Christ, so that we might arrive where he has arrived.[32]

Moralistic tendencies are easily observable in Colet's christology, but that does not mean that Colet predicated the forgiveness of sins exclusively upon the believer's moral improvement. His assertions about Christ's atonement were intended to engage a person's faith while his moral proposition was intended to extend faith into action. Together they were designed to illumine a single *"accesum ad Deum."*[33] Faith in the elimination of sin occasioned by God's compassionate gift of Christ and

---

Padberg, *Erasmus als Katechet* (Freiburg, 1956), p. 157; and James Henry Rieger, "Erasmus, Colet, and the Schoolboy Jesus," *Studies in the Renaissance* 9 (1962): 187-94. For Erasmus's *Carmina*, see Clericus, ed., *Opera omnia Des. Erasmi Roterodami*, 10 vols. (Leiden, 1703-1706), 5:1321.

[32]EEC, p. 206: "[P]artim hic agenda dum hic vivitur; partim expectanda futura. Quae hic agantur, est ex amore boni contentio ad eam rectam vivendi rationem piam et justam, quam in se ipso justus Christus tanquam exemplar nobis representaivit. Quod autem expectatur futurum, est supra modum illud in sublimitate aeternum gloriae pondus, quod talis imitatio Christi operatur in nobis, non contemplantibus quae videntur, sed quae non videntur. Desiderio illius tanti et tam beatifici praemii, anhelo cursu in Christi vestigiis illum sectari debemus antecedentem; ut, quo ille pervenerit, nos perveniamus."

[33]EER-a, p. 279.

by Christ's selfless sacrifice was insufficient without the believer's personal death to sin. Christ not only gave his life for persons estranged from God by virtue of their first ancestor's trespass but also left his life as a model for persons inspired to reconcile themselves to God's will. Colet's moral theology stood fundamentally on the supernatural mediation of God to man in the incarnation and resurrection of Christ, that is, on Christ's perfect divinity. His moral theology turned, however, on Christ's perfect humanity. Christ is *"frater noster"*: he shared our humanity so that he might instruct us in human righteousness. In Colet's understanding, Christ was primarily what William Clebsch has called a "patterning agent," and Colet was thoroughly convinced that the end to sin and the advance of righteousness depended upon persons' attraction to Christ's humanity and not upon their adoration of His divinity.[34]

It appears that Colet sensed no need to formulate some *communicatio idiomatum* with regard to the confluence of perfect humanity and divinity in Jesus Christ. He had little good to say about priests who indulged in idle speculation about the hypostases of the Godhead. For his part, he was willing to confirm the coexistence of Christ's divinity and humanity, but he judged the "how" of coexistence to be a scholastic Hydra: when one aspect of the problem is sliced into a formula, others arise to defy human logic. Moreover, this gloomy inevitability had nothing to do with the advancement of Christ's righteousness. Colet needed no rationally devised principles for the simultaneous predications of divine and human qualities; for what was significant for him was that Christ shared with both God and St. Paul, the quite human apostle, the desire that persons should scrupulously follow the good.[35] Christ's preaching and the apostolic preaching about Christ were oriented to promote moral regeneration and not, as far as Colet could tell, to encourage doctrinal sophistication.[36]

----

[34]EER-b, p. 216; EEC, p. 218; CORP, p. 190; and SAC, p. 65. Also see William Clebsch, "John Colet and Reformation," *Anglican Theological Review* 37 (1955): 169; and C. A. L. Jarrott, "John Colet on Justification," *Sixteenth Century Journal* 7 (1976): 65-66.

[35]EEC, pp. 196, 232-33.

[36]EEC, p. 211: "[C]um agnovimus modo optimum quiddam et perfectissimum in Christo propositum fuisse in terris et hominibus, est intelligendum pro salute omnium consultum esse universis, ut se in illum statum, quo erat Christi, reforment. Nec aliud

At the beginning of the century that was to witness numerous spirited conflicts about what Christ taught, Colet directed attention to how Christ lived. The preeminence of the moral proposition in Colet's christology fits fairly well with what we know of the immense popularity of late medieval *vitae Christi* and devotional manuals.[37] But Colet's moral theology also characterizes the Catholic Reform that preceded the great sixteenth-century controversies. Protests about the sacrament of penance and the proliferation of indulgences would soon swell into a new understanding of justification and a reformation of the church that would break across Europe. Colet, however, in his earliest lectures, offered a modest interpretation of justification: "to the best of your ability, to be as Christ was—this is justification."[38] He was convinced that "if they are willing" (*"si velint"*), persons may live so as to possess eternal life.[39] His conviction keynoted a reform of the church and of the Christian life carried forward by Erasmus, but his conviction and the understanding of justification that braced it still require considerable clarification.

Reshaping Voluntarist Mysticism: A Practical Spirituality

John Colet would not have repeated his words, "to the best of your ability" and "if they are willing," without admitting the absolute and

---

quaesivit vel illius, vel post illum Apostolorum evangelizatio, nisi ut ad exemplar Christi omnium vitae reformentur." Erasmus reported that he engaged Colet in a friendly debate about the natures of Christ. The issue turned on Christ's Gethsemane supplication that his destiny be amended and on the problems posed by this episode for allegations that Christ's propitiatory purpose was steadfast and his divine nature impassible. Erasmus posited two natures and two wills (Clericus, *Opera omnia*, 5:1283). He kept the opposites in tension in order to press the point that divine treasures are always contained in fragile earthen vessels. Colet, it seems, confined his rebuttal to Erasmus's claim that the same scriptural episode permitted equally valid yet vastly different interpretations (Clericus, *Opera omnia*, 5:1291-94). He believed that Christ's humanity was Christ's strength and that the Gethsemane appeal was motivated by compassion for the persecutors and not by an all-too-human fear of death that coexisted with Christ's divine courage (Clericus, *Opera omnia*, 5:1266-67). By denying that weakness (*"imbecillitas"*) was disclosed at Gethsemane, Colet effectively avoided the problem of Christ's apparently contrary attitudes toward his fate. Compassion for an enemy is a common theme in Colet's discussions of *caritas*; see EER-b, pp. 171-72, 194-95; EEC, pp. 168-69, 189.

[37]See Lucien Febvre, *Au coeur réligieux du XVIe siècle* (Paris, 1957), pp. 43-44.

[38]EER-a, p. 242: "Esse talem, quoad poteris, qualis fuerit Christus, justificatio est."

[39]EER-b, p. 151.

indisputable prevenience of grace to any salvific endeavor. Indeed, that kind of admission so characterizes Colet's earliest lectures that his evaluation of both the relative independence of human choice and the importance of human industry is nearly eclipsed. Colet's remarks about grace and human will have been reviewed, especially since the appearance in 1952 of Eugene Rice's penetrating paper on Colet's alleged "annihilation" of the natural order; but virtually no interpretation has gone unopposed, and the reconciliation of Colet's appreciations for the gratuity of grace and for the necessity of human deliberation and effort remains problematic. This is due perhaps to the unanimous disregard in Colet studies for the Englishman's voluntarist mysticism that ransomed Augustine's synergism from medieval scholastic syntheses that codified and recodified it.

If human volition, unaided by grace, were expected to achieve some soteriologically significant measure of moral regeneration, the most likely place to look for guidance would be the sage precepts of the Mosaic laws. It is not surprising that Augustine was especially irritated by the Pelagian argument that the law could be understood as a "grace." For Augustine, grace could be neither legislated nor codified. He sensed that the identification of grace with law might confer eternal life upon anyone who obeyed the Old Testament's commandments apart from the special grace announced in the New Testament's gospel.[40] No matter how praiseworthy, law qua law, according to Augustine, only exacerbated evil desires by forbidding them. Those desires were like a powerful current, and "when an object [here, the law] is placed in its way, it does not cease to flow but its flow is made more forceful. It overflows its customary boundaries and having been hurled by the great mass, it rolls along forward more violently."[41] The law cannot transform evil desire. It may, however, vivify the criminal effects of evil intent and possibly encourage the sinner to confess the limitations of self-will, only thinly disguised as

---

[40]See Augustine's *Contra duas epistolas Pelagianorum*, 4.5.11; and *De spiritu et littera*, 10.16, 18.31, and 19.32.

[41]*De spiritu et littera*, 4.6: "[P]rofecto illa lex, quamvis bona, auget prohibendo desiderium malum: sicut aquae impetus, si in eam partem non cesset influere, vehementior fit obice opposito, cujus molem cum eviceret, majore cumulo praecipitatus violentius per prona provolvitur."

attempts to keep faith with the letter of the law, and to seek help elsewhere. Augustine expected nothing more from the tablets that Moses brought with him from the summit of Sinai.

Colet also pointed out that the law of Moses was bereft of life-giving power. When the apostle occasionally spoke favorably of the Mosaic oracles, he was only speaking in deference to the Jews. For the Christian, the law had little significance. It did, however, fix boundaries to notify evildoers of the sin *contra Deum* involved in their noxious conduct of worldy affairs, but the boundaries were incapable of preventing transgressions. In fact, God had issued prohibitions that humankind was powerless to observe without the special assistance of grace. Colet recognized the law as an instructor ("*pedagogus*") that, at its best, trained individuals in mutual service; but the law's ambitions to regulate human behavior were, without grace, "*frustratum et vacuum.*" Equally vain were human efforts to comply, without grace, with the rigorous precepts of the law. From this circle of frustration, the law promised some deliverance insofar as it disclosed human debilities and its own inadequacy and, therefore compelled humankind to seek a truly skilled physician. "Once the works of the law have been set aside, if someone, be he Jew or Gentile, only work Christ, he will be justified." This remark, set in Colet's first discussion of St. Paul's *per fidem* passage (Romans 3:28), pairs faith and love ("*per fidem quae per dilectionem operatur Christum*") against the ceremonial laws. None of the efforts promoted by the old laws were of the same magnitude as the righteousness inspired by Christ.[42]

Earlier in Colet's first exposition of the third chapter of Romans, grace and will were mentioned together for the first time in the Oxford lectures; and this also in connection with the advice to relinquish the law and to hold fast to Christ. Colet asserted that the carnal Jew can become a spiritual Jew "if he is willing and/or if grace lays hold of him" ("*si voluerit, immo si illum arripuerit gratia*"). "*Immo*" may be taken in one of two ways. It has been translated as if it contradicted that which

---

[42]EER-a, p. 242: "Intelligit sacraficia, ritus, ceremonias, cultumque corporalem; in quo assidui notabili superstitione erant illi veri Judei. His operibus legis omissis, si quispiam operetur Christum, justificabitur, sive Judeus sive gentilis sit; quia non est distinctio: bonus Jesus recipit omnes indifferenter." Also note EER-a, pp. 217, 232, 279; EER-b, pp. 147-48; CORP, pp. 186-88.

precedes it (*"si voluerit"*), that is, as if Colet wished immediately to countermand his inclusion of human volition in the pursuit of righteousness. The context, however, appears to substantiate another rendering, for Colet spoke as if the Jews could participate in their own transformations. "If they discarded the image [the law], they could yet be claimed by the Truth itself [Jesus Christ]." Colet followed this with an elaborate denial that anyone might frustrate God's purpose, but he nowhere foreclosed on the possibility that one might cooperate with it. The Jew then, according to Colet, could turn away from the inflated claims of the law "if he is willing and indeed if grace lays hold of him."[43]

Other passages in Colet's earliest lecture reinforce the impression that he entertained some notion of human will's importance. He conceded that the "gentle encouragement" of the New Testament elicits a "free and voluntary" response and that the justifying faith that should be forthcoming requires "fellow working" with Christ and in imitation of him.[44] Select phrases, of course, do not yield conclusive testimony to Colet's determination to coordinate grace and will from the beginning of his Oxford career. Nevertheless, they indicate a clear appreciation of the importance of human volition that increasingly became a factor in the development of his soteriology. Human effort, assisted somehow by grace, was necessary to disengage the Christian from those powers that constrict the proper operation of will and intellect.[45]

In places, Colet appears to think that grace's early help is negligible and that the preliminary disengagement from distractions and temptation was, in the strictest sense, meritorious. "God is patient," Colet declared in his first lecture on Romans 2:7. "He waits and waits for men to repent. . . . [A]nd toward those who have been made gentle and penitent, He is immediately gentle and compassionate. Without further ado, He forgives them and, afterward, as they continue to act well, He gives them glory, honor, immortality, and peace."[46] The second chapter

---

[43]EER-a, p. 223. Note Lupton's translation, p. 96.

[44]EER-a, pp. 244, 248.

[45]See, for example, EER-a, p. 236; EER-b, pp. 150, 164; EEC, pp. 167, 191-93.

[46]EER-a, p. 215: "Bonitate enim sua patiens, benignus, et longanimis est. Expectat diu ut homines peniteant. . . . Revera mollibus et penitentibus statim mollis et misericors est

of St. Paul's letter to Rome leaves the impression that works of righteousness play a major role in justification, but Colet seems to have acquired a special fondness for the idea that good works elicit divine mercy. His undated treatise on the sacraments reiterated briefly the "rewards system" that appeared but once in his earliest lecture: "When God sees confession, penance, and satisfaction . . . He righteously shows compassion and He mercifully justifies."[47] Elsewhere, however, and particularly in his Oxford lectures, Colet left no doubt that human righteousness can make no claim upon divine liberality and that a gracious God only bestows his gifts gratuitously. God's grace is the prerequisite for justification and for the believer's righteousness. Acknowledgment of the gift of grace prevenient to all worthy human activity was, for Colet as it was for Augustine, the *conditio sine qua non* for any salutary relationship between man and God. Grace is not then a consolation to be won or lost but rather the essential resource for self-management that God's redemptive design requires.[48]

Humankind could not press its own case before the ultimate bar of justice; nor could it "earn" divine mercy. The first possibility was excluded by humanity's complicity in its own sinfulness and disorder. Self-will could not be overcome by self-will. The second possibility rested on a terminological contradiction: "earned" mercy was not mercy, but rather justice. Colet concluded that human volition could have no direct influence on the efficacy of grace, but he was equally sure that grace was not a coercive force, an infusion that suddenly added to an immovable, iron will some aptitude for righteousness. The stalemate might have paralyzed Colet, had he not been supremely confident both that will could somehow seek its way out of disorder and that grace could somehow assist that preliminary discretion toward righteousness. Instead, the stalemate issued in a fresh resolution of the problem of grace and will.

Deus, ac facile ignoscit, atque postremo bene operantibus reddet gloriam et honorem, incorruptionem et pacem."

[47]SAC, p. 86: "[C]onfessionem cum videt peccatorum, poenitentiam, ac satisfactionem, tum miseretur juste et misericorditer justificat."

[48]Colet would not have disputed Augustine's appraisal of St. Paul as *"constantissimus gratiae praedicator"* (*De spiritu et littera*, 13.22). See, inter alia, EER-a, pp. 229, 239, 251-53; EER-b, pp. 168, 173-75, 190, 229; EEC, p. 219.

Colet stipulated that grace draws the will ever so gently that the will could be said to follow the lead of grace "naturally." Divine grace had a special way of conforming to nature without relinquishing the essential quality of grace, namely, gratuity. Indeed (*"immo!"*) nature herself could not be any more gentle or any more "natural" than the sure but light touch of God's grace on human will.[49] The human will is not simply a collaborator but also the chief locus of collaboration between God and man, a coalition that was actually a conflation (*"coiens"*) of wills that enabled the Christian to deliver himself (*"se solvens"*) from the grip of self-will and sin.

The parenthetical expressions in the previous sentence are drawn from Colet's treatise on the sacraments. There he explained that "God despatches to man the will to acknowledge . . . and to cast off his sins," but that the sacrament of penance refers not only to the remission that God has granted but also to the contrition and righteousness actively pursued by two agents as one. Indeed, the sacraments attest to the confluence of divine and human wills (*"testes et foedera coeuntium voluntatis"*), that is, to "the divine will established in man and [to] human will established in God."[50] It was axiomatic for Thomas Aquinas and for many who followed him that grace respected and preserved nature, and scholasticism was not at all inarticulate about the relation between grace and human volition. Colet, however, was a scholastic *manqué*, more adept at proclaiming than at explaining the reconciliation. Perhaps he returned to Augustine for whom the transformation of the will (from *nolens* to *volens*) was accomplished from within the will. Colet, as Augustine, took Philippians 2:13 ("It is God who works in you") to mean that God mysteriously works *nobiscum* as well as *in nobis*.[51]

The *De sacramentiis ecclesiae* lifted the problem above scholastic

---

[49]EER-b, pp. 161-62; EEC, p. 223.

[50]SAC, pp. 89-91. Early church expositions of baptismal and penitential practices were favorite places for discussions of works and of their soteriological importance. See *Dictionnaire de théologie catholique*, s.v. "Justification," (J. Rivière), 8:2089.

[51]See Augustine, *De diversis quaestionibus ad Simplicianum*, 1.2.12; and *Contra duas epistolas Pelagianorum*, 1.19.37. For Aquinas, however, Philippians 2:13 seemed to confirm God's movement of the will *"sicut ab exteriori principio."* See the *Summa theologiae*, 1a 2ae, 9.6.

contention by setting its solution in the language of voluntarist mysticism. By any measure, the terms are unscientific. They indicate Colet's discrete indifference to the scholarly disputes about prevenient graces and partial merit (that is, *meritum de congruo*) as well as his willingness to import the pseudo-Dionysius's "theology of mediation" to mitigate the dualism implicit in some Pauline concepts. The treatise on the sacraments is undated, but it probably followed Colet's close reading of pseudo-Dionysius and was written after Colet left Oxford to assume his duties as Dean of St. Paul's in London. For the pseudo-Dionysius, angels mediate God to humanity, the church mediates the celestial order to the terrestrial, apostles mediate Christ to Christians as vital spirits mediate the soul to the body. In each instance, the mediator is the point at which divine and human coincide, the former to impress its likeness upon the latter. In such a context, Colet could sketch free human choice as the point at which God's unlimited capacity to promote human righteousness was mediated to each individual's feeble capacity to redeem the disorders that he occasioned. The way had been cleared, however, in Colet's Oxford lectures and with his understanding of practical spirituality for the resolution pronounced in the *De sacramentis*. In fact, in the lectures, one can trace the development of Colet's voluntarist mysticism.

The prolegomena to Colet's very first set of lectures appealed to St. Paul's definition of the Holy Spirit, which, in Colet's restatement, took on a distinctly functional, as opposed to speculative, nature.

> The Spirit of sanctification, as St. Paul calls it, is the Holy Spirit of God which sanctifies and vivifies, makes one pleasing to God, and makes peace with God. It is, therefore, grace and the peace of men that proceeds from both the Father and the Son and that St. Paul often desires for those to whom he writes. The Holy Spirit is the worshipful love of God. It makes men lovers and loveable with regard to both God and neighbors, self and others—all in God's love.[52]

---

[52]EER-a, p. 202: "Spiritus sanctificationis, ut hic Paulus vocat, spiritus ipse est sanctus Dei, qui sanctificat, vivificat, gratificat, pacificat Deo. Ideo gratia est et pax hominum, quae procedit pariter a Patre et a Filio; quam totiens Paulus optat eis ad quos scribit. Is ipse venerandus amor est Dei, amantificans homines, faciensque eos amabiles tum Deo tum hominibus, et sibi et aliis, in amore Dei."

The ministration of love was the true miracle of the Holy Spirit and the most complete form of its self-disclosure. Spirit brings the possibility of a new life (*"vivificat"*) and a new relatedness to God (*"pacificat Deo"*). Divine inspiration, for Colet, was not to be kept imprisoned in the worshipful but solitary life of the believer. To be sure, the *incendium amoris* inspires not only love for God but also an active righteousness that spreads God's love to the neighbor (*"amantificans homines"*). By speaking of active righteousness in connection with the functions of the Holy Spirit, Colet tacitly raised the question of the believer's role in spiritual animation and salvation. Although, as has been documented, his earliest lectures demonstrate his appreciation for human volition and human effort in redemptive actions, only in his second set of lectures on Romans did Colet set that appreciation in the context of his understanding of spirituality.

Where St. Paul noted that sons of God were "led by the Spirit" (Romans 8:14), Colet called to mind the injunction in the apostle's letter to Galatians (5:25) to "walk in the Spirit"; and then he listed the duties and privileges of Christians *"notati et . . . insigniti spiritu sancto."* Colet's inference is clear: possibilities for a new life afforded by the Spirit must be actualized by the believer. In his second exposition of Romans, therefore, he treated St. Paul's doctrine of the Spirit as an exhortation to perseverance in the righteous life. He divided inspiration into two "subprocesses." First, the Holy Spirit alters the very form of human faculties (*"nova hominis et spiritualis forma"*); then, mutatis mutandis, the activity of the Christian becomes that of the Spirit (*"novae vires et verae et potentes"*). Colet was not always diligent in keeping the two "subprocesses" distinct and the second dependent upon the first. A reading of his second and third sets of lectures on Romans gives the impression of a pendulum-like movement between discussions of the ordering of one's faculties and discussions of the reordering of one's life. Indeed, "spiritual being," as Colet in a separate treatise referred to the alteration of faculties, often melded with "spiritual working," that is, inspired human activity.[53]

The precise nature of God's work in the believer, the infusion of

---

[53]Compare EER-b, pp. 152-53 and 166-67 with CORP, p. 189.

spiritual form, remained, for Colet, an impenetrable mystery. One only ascertains "spiritual being" from the inexorable flow of spiritual, and therefore, righteous actions that comprise the new life and bear witness to the new relatedness to God offered by the Holy Spirit. When Colet later reminded a 1512 convocation of clergy of St. Paul's words, "Be not conformed to this world, but be reformed in the newness of your understanding" (Romans 12:2), he spoke of the newness of the faculty only by schematizing its implications for conduct.[54] He tackled the same passage in his second set of lectures and with the same results. The spiritual reformation of the faculty is perceptible as a new "sense and judgment about things," namely, a moral transvaluation that arises from spiritual transformation and that is, itself, understood as a whole constellation of new and spiritual attitudes and actions.[55] This is tantamount to a concession that, save for "spiritual working," the infusion of spiritual form is undetectable. This, in turn, means that the objective reality of the Holy Spirit and its ministrations to the believer can only be known through the human subject as that which the Spirit "leads" but also as that which is an agent in its own right.

This schematization, however, leaves a significant question unanswered. If the flow of "spiritual working" is inexorable, how can one speak of the subject as an agent "in its own right"? Is there some small scrap of volition or deliberation that might be attributed to the believer's own righteousness? The question might be put more clearly by exploring the justification in Colet's thought for considering the human will as subject rather than as object or instrument. Colet, however, anticipated the question and confronted in his lectures on Corinthians the troublesome issue of human agency. Authentic spirituality, he claimed, was not achieved as long as the Spirit merely acted upon man. In that case, the will would be but a dead instrument ("*mortuum organum*"), something that is not to be confused with the living instrument ("*vivum organum et*

---

[54]CONV, pp. 294-303. The text of Colet's sermon has been republished in two recent anthologies of Renaissance and Reformation literature: John C. Olin, ed., *The Catholic Reformation, Savonarola to Ignatius* (New York, 1969), pp. 27-39; and Lewis Spitz, ed., *The Northern Renaissance* (Englewood Cliffs, New Jersey, 1972), pp. 110-21.

[55]EER-b, p. 176.

instrumentum") that Colet classified as a "coagent" with the Holy Spirit. The change is possible because love of God and neighbor so inflames the believer that he himself "does all things in the Spirit—not, as before, the Spirit in [him]." Instrumentality does not then preclude subjectivity. Quite the contrary, genuine subjectivity and righteousness presuppose what might be termed an inspired instrumentality.[56] The human will became a coefficient cause of righteousness, prompted by the example of Christ and the presence of the Holy Spirit.

The vindication of human agency in Colet's soteriology is the day by day growth in righteousness that was constituent of spirituality.[57] Justification was not exclusively identified with the Spirit's infusion of form, with the reception in faith of God's promises, or with the grace of baptism. Baptism itself counted for nothing, in Colet's judgment, unless it was followed by strict adherence to the gospel, that is, by steady advance in patience, humility, and love, which required discipline and effort as well as divine assistance.[58]

The spiritual life prescribed by St. Paul and outlined by Colet was nothing other than this steady advance. Colet did not, however, naively suppose that the unsettling eruptions of self-will could easily and suddenly be silenced. Righteousness was a constant struggle, relieved only, it appeared to Colet, by Christ's promise of victory. Colet's lectures mixed contest imagery with St. Paul's more forthright exhortations to virtue, and he freely admitted the possibility of backsliding. In this context a strictly predestinarian understanding of election would be unintelligible, and yet in Colet's second set of lectures on Romans he introduced that perspective, apparently without any sense that it might be somewhat out of place and therefore objectionable.

---

[56]EEC, p. 257: "Et ipse tum ista omnia agis in spiritu; nedum in te spiritus, sicuti antea. Disponit agens in formam; res formata deinque per se agit"; EEC, p. 259: "Alia mortua organa, non edificata ipsa, nonnunquam forsan edificant vel ipsa inflata. In illis operatur spiritus solus. In his homo, jam vivum organum et instrumentum, et ex corpore, cum spiritu cooperatur, dono sibi dato, in virtute spiritus, causae et agentis exemplaris, et animae corporis, et architecti domus Dei, id est, ecclesiae. . . . Cui [Spiritus Dei] famulantur, serviunt et obediunt homines, vivificati et perfecti charitate, ut causae organicae et instrumentales."

[57]EEC, p. 266; SAC, pp. 82-83.

[58]EER-a, p. 227; EEC, pp. 205-206.

That John Colet steadfastly confirmed active righteousness as a spiritual struggle and as the result of the coalition between divine and human wills and that he also set forth the divine verdict as irreversible presents something of a problem. There seems to be no way to avoid the collision between his many discussions of righteousness and his single but lengthy excursus on predestination. One can only hope, by way of a conclusion, to find meanings in Colet's doctrine of predestination and in his conceptualization of the Christian life that will absorb much of the impact of the collision and preserve the logic of his *ordo salutis*.

Minimally, the defense of predestination involved an affirmation of divine sovereignty. Colet judged that St. Paul's doctrines of election and predestination could be compressed into a single and "minimal" proposition: whatever affects the blessedness of man is contingent upon God's will and grace. He contended that the irrevocability of divine judgment was only crucial to the apostle's soteriology in the sense that irrevocability properly humbled the Jews who pretended that their observances elicited predictable divine responses. The obligation to reward this or that act would prove the undoing of divine sovereignty over the order of salvation, so St. Paul's strategy, as Colet understood it, was to advance his case for the supremacy of God's will in the form of rather rigid doctrines of election and predestination. Colet's own doctrines were nothing more than repetitions of what he took to have been the apostle's case and explanations of the circumstances that occasioned it.[59] St. Paul had cautioned against questioning the technical ways and means of God's will (Romans 9:20), and Colet respected the limits that this admonition seemed to set upon inquiry. The undefined and, for Colet, indefinite "how" and "why" of predestination added to the mystique of God's sovereignty.[60] But the mystery of election, though an affirmation of God's supreme, though unfathomable, judgment, did not preclude the coalition in which God and the Christian could be said to be partners in righteousness. The irreversibility of election might well be conditional. Colet terminated his defense of predestination and election when he was satisfied that St. Paul's "minimal" proposition had been established, that

---

[59]EER-b, pp. 163-68.

[60]EER-b, pp. 159-60.

is, when he had reaffirmed that God supervised and grace permeated the order of salvation.[61] His own notion of backsliding, however, not only discloses the steady hand of God in the Christian's pursuit of righteousness but also attests to the probability that Colet advocated conditional election and predestination even in his extended commentary on St. Paul's arguments.

Colet believed that the full weight of prior sinfulness returned to the believer who was not steadfast in the pursuit of righteousness. In addition to the cumulative burden of previous sins, the backslider must suffer the consequences of having sinned after receiving divine forgiveness and presumably the assistance of the Holy Spirit.[62] Colet guessed that the fate of one who forsakes righteousness was far worse than that of one who never knew righteousness, and, at one point, he predicted that backsliding would so increase the culprit's guilt that return to divine favor would be highly unlikely.[63]

At first glance, this hard-line approach to backsliding and the alleged finality of divine reprobation seems as much a menace as the apparent irreversibility of election to the doctrine of the Christian life that Colet proposed elsewhere. If God so severely penalized the cracks and flaws in human conduct, only saints would be Christians. More to the point, this stern interpretation of divine judgment delivers mortal blows both to active righteousness and to divine sovereignty, for the backslider's ability to derail his own salvation would be deemed greater than the power of grace to reroute it. Colet, therefore, conceded that many of his remarks on the topic of backsliding had been intended to frighten the potential wrongdoer.[64] G. R. Owst observed "a charming disregard of the risks of

---

[61]Hugh Latimer's advice is representative of later English indifference to the subtleties of the debate about predestination that preoccupied continental theologians. "So we need not go about to trouble ourselves with curious questions of the predestination of God. But let us rather endeavor ourselves that we may be in Christ . . . then we may be sure that we are ordained to everlasting life." See the *Sermons and Remains of Hugh Latimer*, ed. George Elwes Corrie, The Parker Society Publications, vols. 27 and 28 (Cambridge, 1844-45), 28:175. Latimer was one of the few sixteenth-century reformers who publicly honored the memory of John Colet (27:440).

[62]EER-a, p. 247; EER-b, p. 153.

[63]EER-b, pp. 144-45.

[64]EER-b, pp. 145-46.

inconsistency" in late medieval preaching. The same homily might first threaten sinners with eternal damnation and then comfort them with the thought of eternal mercy.[65] Colet appears to have been aware of the forensic utility of the notion of irrevocable condemnation, and he shaped his declarations as a deterrent to discourage backsliding but not to discourage the penitent backslider. Penance, struggle, and forgiveness were, for him, the hallmarks of the spiritual life. God's door was open to the prodigal: "If you rise up rapidly, even though you are not to be compared with those who never fall, inasmuch as you are not willing to 'take it lying down,' you are a useful soldier."[66]

Colet understood that backsliding was no more uncommon in the Christian life than advance, so his theories of divine election and predestination must have included conditional clauses even when they appeared absolute. Despite his prolonged restatement of St. Paul's position that appeared to favor unconditional predestination, Colet retained throughout his life commitments to furnish traction for the Christian's advance in righteousness and to dramatize the terrifying consequences of retrogression. He fulfilled the first by proclaiming the assistance available to the sincere but feeble human will. He fulfilled the second commitment not only by proffering the notion of final rebuke but also by identifying behavioral lapses with doctrinal infidelities and by classifying them both with the dreaded term "heresy." He linked backsliding to schism and he redefined "unbelief" as failure to profess one's faith in deeds. To a convocation of clergy called to extirpate doctrinal irregularities, Colet preached against irregularities in clerical conduct, stigmatizing them as the most treacherous kind of heresy. The point of all this was to relate faith and doctrine to life and to make the deplorable prospect of a break in the cadence of Christian advance in the pursuit of righteousness especially remote.[67]

Following Marsilio Ficino, whom he tremendously admired, Colet thought of *justitia* as a moral virtue. In place of the perfunctorily per-

---

[65]G. R. Owst, *Preaching in Medieval England* (Cambridge, 1926), pp. 334-36, 346-47.

[66]SAC, p. 87: "Statim si resurgas, quanquam non es comparandus cum illis qui nunquam ceciderint, tamen cum nolis victus jacere, miles non es inutilis."

[67]CONV, pp. 298-99; EER-a, pp. 226-27; EER-b, p. 193; EEC, p. 242.

formed oblations that he criticized in his earliest lectures, he suggested a "sacrifice of righteousness" ("*sacrificium justitiae*") as the proper offering to God.[68] His lectures on Romans portray the spiritual life as a self-oblation in which the Christian dedicates works of righteousness to God and becomes "a living sacrifice" ("*viva hostia*"), morally responsible because he is righteous and righteous because he is morally responsible.[69]

Strictly speaking, the moral life does not merit righteousness; nor does righteousness precede and produce moral responsibility. But what from one angle appears to be unbroken circularity, from another angle gives the correct impression of a perfect identification of moral and soteriological concerns in John Colet's lectures. In his very first lecture he averred that genuine Christianity ("*vera Christianitas*") was synonymous with full and perfect righteousness ("*pl[ena] perfectaque justitia*"), that is, with "a contempt of worldliness, an ardent desire for heavenly things, patience in the face of all evils, and all kinds of good deeds performed at all times, for all persons, in the sight of God, with the fear of God, and for a heavenly reward." That idea developed and was complemented by the notion of divine and human collaboration, by the moral proposition of Colet's christology, and by an increasingly sharp focus on spirituality. Throughout his lectures, however, Colet displayed his conviction that "*in actione emicant omnia*," righteousness shows itself in the Christian life.[70] It remains now to set this understanding of Colet alongside his reputation as a church reformer and to locate his rightful place in the history of the Christian traditions.

---

[68]See Ficino, *Opera omnia*, 1:633; and MARG, 20, p. 95 and 31, p. 100. Also review EER-a, pp. 209, 215-16, 221 and SAC, p. 77.

[69]See EER-a, p. 250; EER-b, pp. 177-78.

[70]EER-a, p. 241: "[Q]uae justitiae, ut summatim dicam, constitit in contemptu terrenorum, et ardenti desiderio coelestium; in patientia omnis mali; in actione omnis boni, in omni tempore, et ad omnes, coram Deo, in timore illius, pro mercede coelesti." Also see EEC, p. 265.

4   *"Be Reformed . . .*
That You May Prove God's Will"

John Colet's university lectures and later treatises set his notions of church reform and church order in the context of his soteriology in a way that made him a chief creditor of the Catholic Reformation. Paolo Brezzi's conjecture that "a vast circle of reformers" gathered around Colet at Oxford is altogether untrue and it probably derived from an uncritical reading of Frederic Seebohm's more ambitious remarks about an "Oxford Reformation."[1] But among those Catholics, scholastics, humanists, mendicants, and mystics, whose discontent with church government preceded and perhaps shaped later and more outspoken protests, John Colet deserves a special place.

Presently, Colet's reputation as a church reformer rests principally on the sermon that he delivered to the clergy of England's Southern Province (Canterbury) assembled in 1512 at St. Paul's Cathedral at the request of Archbishop William Warham. It is Colet's only surviving sermon, but it would not be unfair to speculate that it was among his most rebellious. His colleagues were convened to consider measures against various forms of disbelief and heresy, but Colet seized the occasion to

---

[1]Paolo Brezzi, *Le Riforme Cattoliche dei secolo XV e XVI* (Rome, 1945), p. 39. Brezzi's identification and classification of the Catholic reform, especially as it relates to the Counterreformation (pp. 96-97), are exceptionally useful. Also consult, however, Hubert Jedin's refinements, *Katholische Reformation oder Gegenreformation* (Lucerne, 1946).

warn them of the ruin of the church brought on by their own misconduct. Any examination of righteousness and reformation in Colet's thought must begin with this homily and with its place in the history of the impulse toward self-reformation in English Catholicism. Colet's reformist sympathies, however, cannot be unraveled from this single sermon.[2] St. Paul and the pseudo-Dionysius shaped his understandings of church and churchmanship that developed along with his soteriology from his earliest Oxford lectures. For Colet, St. Paul set forth normative standards for the conduct of church life and anchored his moral theology with the ideal of church unity. The pseudo-Dionysius set the moralism of his alleged mentor into an appropriately ordered institutional framework, an ecclesiastical hierarchy modeled after the structure of the cosmos and according to the revealed will of God. Hence the discussion of this chapter turns from Colet's famous sermon to the sources of his ecclesiology and to the manner in which they have been employed to integrate the ideas of unity, order, and righteousness with Colet's general call for a reform of church life.

The conduct of church affairs was important to Colet not only because a sound church was a clear and agreeable sign of the personal righteousness of its officials and its members but also because the church itself was an agent in the promotion of Christian righteousness.[3] To accuse and insult the neighbor is to repel the stranger. Outsiders are attracted to righteousness by the practice of righteousness. When Colet spoke of the church's role *in propagatione justitiae*, however, proselytism was not foremost in his intention. His point was that the soteriological effective-

---

[2]August Humbert's contention that the sermon marks Colet's self-conscious shift from doctrine and its reformulation to church life and its reform is highly questionable. See Humbert's *Les Origines de la théologie moderne* (Paris, 1911), p. 143. The solemn separation of the two concerns reflects the vast tradition in scholarship that has either found little place for Catholic reformers before Ignatius and Trent or misunderstood reformers as theological mavericks and proto-Lutherans or as "mere moralists." Also note Michael J. Kelly's arguments for the sermon's earlier delivery (1510), "Canterbury Jurisdiction and Influence During the Episcopate of William Warham," Ph.D. Dissertation, Cambridge University, 1963, p. 112. Though inconclusive, Kelly's position has not wanted weighty endorsement, e.g., G. R. Elton, *Reform and Reformation* (Cambridge, 1977), p. 57.

[3]SAC, p. 63.

ness of righteousness presupposed its moral effectiveness, which, in turn, required the exercise of volition in a social context. And it can be argued, as it will be argued here, that whereas St. Paul and the pseudo-Dionysius were sources for Colet's ecclesiology, the mainspring of his concern for the church's reform was his soteriology and the place of honor he reserved for the notion of active righteousness. The church must be a place where righteousness is taught and practiced or neither churchman nor outsider can be saved. In a sense, the church became for Colet a proving ground, the final test of both the moral and soteriological effectiveness of righteousness that consists in the maintenance of order, unity, and reform as constant features of church life. The final purpose of this review of Colet's thought is to demonstrate how his understanding of reform is fundamentally and systematically linked with his adaptation of the Augustinian soteriological tradition.

"Evyll Teachynge" and "Evyll Example"

Misbehavior among the clergy had been material for Oxford lectures and treatises since the days of John Wyclif. Although Wyclif nearly ended the era in which one might criticize the church without seeming to be heterodox, the less spectacular career of Chancellor Gascoigne at Oxford in the middle of the fifteenth century is proof that criticism was not automatically associated with disloyalty. John Bromyard, for example, was not only the most formidable adversary of Lollardy of his time but also a persistent critic of the absenteeism common among God's best paid deputies. Christopher Saint-German contended that clerical ignorance and incontinence had reached scandalous, if not catastrophic, proportions; but even his opponent in a brief but barbed pamphlet exchange, Thomas More, refused to read Saint-German out of the church. Furthermore, More himself conceded that the maladies diagnosed by Saint-German were lamentable; he disputed the significance and pervasiveness but not the existence of abuses of clerical prerogatives. More must have known of the great numbers of poorly trained men admitted into the priesthood when he mused about his Utopia where "they have priests of exceeding holiness, and therefore very few."[4]

---

[4]*The Utopia of Sir Thomas More*, ed. J. H. Lupton (Oxford, 1895), pp. 282-83; and *The Apologye of Syr Thomas More, Knyght*, ed. Arthur Irving Taft (London, 1930).

Thomas More's veiled and cautious criticism and Saint-German's outcry were part of the final act of the Catholic reform in England. Henry VIII and his lieutenant, Thomas Cromwell, seized upon clerical malpractices as excuses for predominantly political purposes and they altered the course of British ecclesiastical history. But more than thirty years before the Henrician Reformation toppled papal authority, closed the monasteries, and (briefly) flirted with continental Protestant theologies, one man predicted that a church staffed with unworthy personnel would be an easy target for its enemies and an unsafe sanctuary for its friends like Thomas More.

Bromyard and Gascoigne in the fifteenth century and Saint-German and More in the sixteenth voiced what must have been widespread disenchantment with clerical misconduct. Colet, whose career began in one century in Gascoigne's Oxford and ended in the next in More's London, had been equally troubled by the comportment of the clergy. His Oxford lectures complained of avarice, worldliness, and malevolence that had earned the putatively spiritual estate a dangerously bad reputation.[5] But the assortment of complaints and accusations in Colet's lectures and later treatises may be taken as a preamble to his most sustained scolding of his colleagues, the 1512 "reformation sermon."

Moral decline in the church must have appeared rapid to Colet for him to risk official disapprobation with a public declamation against his colleagues. His previous charges were of a rather general nature, although they lacked nothing in aggressiveness. "In the name of Christianity," he elsewhere stated, "the greater part of mankind become pagans."[6] By 1512 Colet had derived a decidedly ill temper from observing this paganization, and in his sermon he isolated its cause as "the facion of secular and worldly lyvyng in clerkes and prestes." The clergy had disfigured the church by conforming to the world. They had emptied

---

Saint-German's treatise "Concernynge the division between the spiritualitie and temporalitie," the piece that prompted More's *Apologye*, is conveniently printed in Taft's appendix, pp. 203-53. Consult, as well, editorial introductions to volumes 4 and 9, *The Yale Edition of the Complete Works of St. Thomas More*.

[5]See, for example, EER-a, pp. 243, 279-80; EEC, pp. 185-89.

[6]SAC, p. 75: "[N]unc quoque sub ipso nomine Christianitatis maxima pars hominum paganizet."

the apostle's instructions to the Roman church (Romans 12) of all meaning, so Colet returned there, particularly to St. Paul's call for reform and concomitant warning against conformity, in order to state the theme of his own "reformation" sermon. "Be not conformed to this world, but be reformed in the newness of your understanding, that you may prove what is God's will." Colet began with an itemization of clerical conformity. "Pride," "carnall concupiscence," "secular business," and "worldly covetuousness" not only prevented "clerkes and prestes" from obeying God's will but also imperiled the independence of the church and its usefulness as an agent in the salvation of souls.

Colet classed the nasty habits of his colleagues as "carnall concupiscence." Feasting, hunting, and "sportes and playes" were mixed with more loathsome sensual extravagances in Colet's indictment, which has earned him a reputation as an ascete and puritan. Colet, however, was more interested in what might be termed the lost honesty and spirituality of his profession than in the more or less sensational misbehavior of individuals. His line of attack actually began with his criticism of the inordinate appetite for status and notoriety that sent clerics reeling from one benefice to the next in neglect of their pastoral obligations. At the heart of the problem, according to Colet, was a "devilisshe pride," which compelled God's would-be servants to exchange "the humble bysshoprike of christe" for "the high lordship and power of the worlde."[7] More precisely, Colet charged first that his colleagues had busied themselves with politics to the neglect of their proper duties and second that they treated the church as a business and that their entrepreneurial transactions interfered with their redemptive roles in God's plan for the salvation of souls and, in fact, alienated Christians from the church and from their own salvation.

The first charge, elaborated under the classification of "secular business," was foreshadowed in Colet's first set of lectures. There he alleged that the church was to be above and beyond the jurisdiction of the world's courts, but he knew then as well as in 1512 that his perspective was unpopular. Of the bishops resident in England, many had come to the episcopate from secular service to the king. There was not, to Colet's

---

[7]CONV, p. 295.

regret, a Thomas Becket among them, which is to say that they had never left the king's service. Nominees for ecclesiastical preferment were dedicated to the royal and secular prerogatives that secured them their offices and were practiced in politics. They perpetuated the worldliness and, therefore, the weakness of the church.[8] At one point Colet ventured that the selection of the church's officers by lot, according to ancient practices, would yield results more conducive to piety than the results achieved by the appointment of persons too close to worldly affairs and too committed to personal political advantage. H. C. Porter cites Colet's remarks to this effect and concludes that Colet's primary concern was the intrusion of temporal princes and prerogatives in the life of the church. But Porter fails to cite the phrase that reveals the very heart of Colet's complaint. Colet advised against this intrusion because the selection of leaders of the church was not made with pious intent, *"non humilibus et piis animis, sed superbis et temerariis."*[9] Colet was not as uncompromising with respect to the inviolability of clerical privileges as Porter assumes. As his 1512 sermon indicates, Colet desired that virtue become the sole reason for promotion within the church. The moral quality of the clergy was the sure antidote against the poisons of secular interference with and "secular business" within the church and the talisman that could prevent further erosion of the confidence in the church. The network of lies that, in Colet's judgment, corrupted human nature had superimposed on the governance of the secular estate must not be allowed to replace the spirituality and sacrifice set forth by St. Paul as the recognizable characteristics of church life and service.[10]

---

[8]EER-a, pp. 206-207, 263.

[9]PSD, p. 246; and H. C. Porter, "The Gloomy Dean and the Law: John Colet, 1466-1519," *Essays in Modern English Church History in Memory of Norman Sykes*, ed. G. V. Bennett and J. D. Walsh (Oxford, 1966), pp. 29-33. Porter's conclusions are based on a selective reading of Colet's complaints (PSD, pp. 244-47). For Colet, *libertas ecclesiae* was not something to be legislated but to be earned. "Ye wyll have the churches liberte, and nat to be drawen afore secular juges: and that also is ryght. For hit is in the psalmes: 'Touche ye nat myne anoynted.' But if ye desire this liberte, first unlouse your selfe frome the worldlye bondage, and from the services of men; and lyfte up your selfe frome the worldlye bondage, and from the services of men; and lyfte up your selfe in to the trewe lybertie . . . and serve you God, and raygne in hym. And than, beleve me, the people wyll nat touche the anoynted of theyr Lorde God" (CONV, p. 303).

[10]CONV, p. 300.

Colet's second charge appears even more damaging than the first. While his criticism of "secular business" must have come as a slap in the face to persons who dabbled in politics and who would not have severed so strictly the regulation of church life from the politics of the realm, Colet's complaints about "worldly covetuousness" amounted to an accusation of gross irresponsibility in the government of the church. Pride and concupiscence were essentially private manifestations of conformity. The worst that could be said of "secular business" was that it encouraged the wrong kind of ambition in the church leadership and brought the church perilously close to the interests of the state. The final aspect of clerical conformity, "worldly covetuousness," caused greatest dissension in the church. The quality of church life might outlast the unspiritual concerns of certain ecclesiastical officials and their neglect of their pastoral calling, but covetuousness was the single plague that the first fruits of God's redemptive order were less likely to survive. Covetuousness was, in Colet's terms, "the mother of all iniquitie" insofar as it set aside the proper clerical obligations to discover and implement moral values and to amend "the manners" of Christians in favor of the preoccupation with personal wealth. Tithes, inflated mortuaries, delapidations, sequestrations, and the general claims of ecclesiastical jurisdiction over personal property enshrined in church custom, if not in law, the clergy's unforgivable desires for pecuniary gain.[11]

The church had become, in Colet's estimation, an extension of the profane marketplace. He charged that the cathedral clergy of St. Paul's "desert divine worship . . . turn the common goods to their own personal uses . . . to plunder the church and to make themselves richer."[12] This moral collapse not only led to financial oppression but it also displayed a pattern of self-concern and incontinence that reached from the perverse

---

[11]CONV, p. 296. Also note EER-b, p. 224; and the uncharacteristic irony of Colet's reply to Erasmus's frequent requests for subsidy, Allen, 1:470-71.

[12]"Epitome of the Statutes of the Cathedral, Drawn up by Dean Colet," *Registrum statutorum et consuetudinem ecclesiae cathedralis Sancti Pauli Londinensis*, ed. W. Sparrow Simpson (London, 1873), p. 229: "[D]ivinum cultum relinquunt, curam Ecclesiae abjiciunt; propria lucra sectantur; communia bona in privatos usus vertunt: nec aliud est in hac infelicitate et confusione temporum in Ecclesia Cathedrali residere, quam proprium commodum quaerere; ac ut planius loquar, spoliare Ecclesiam, et se ditiores facere."

shepherd into the lives of his flock. "Lay people have great occasion of evils and cause to fall when those men whose dutie is to drawe men from the affection of this world, by their continual conversation in this worlde teche men to love this worlde, and of the love of the worlde cast them heedlyng in to hell."[13]

Other evils that befall the church, for example, the persecution of tyrants or the apostasy and defection of heretics, have had salutary effects upon the community of true believers. From Colet's perspective, tribulation and doctrinal upheaval, even to the point of schism, appeared as parts of a strategy divinely engineered to strengthen the church and to foster solidarity and cunning among the faithful. Conformity and especially convetuousness were another matter altogether.

> We are also nowe a dayes greved of heretykes, men mad with marveylous folysshenes. But the heresies of them are not so pestilent and pernicious unto us and the people, as the evyll and wicked lyfe of pristes; the whiche, if we believe saynt Barnard, is a certeyn kynde of heresye, and chiefe of all and most perillous. For that same holy father ... preachynge unto the pristes of his tyme ... sayde ... 'There be many catholyke and faithfull men in speakynge and preachynge, the whiche same men are heretykes in workyng. For that that heretykes do by evyll teachynge, that same do they throughe evyll example: they leade the people oute of the ryght way, and brynge them in to errour of lyfe. And so moche they are worse than heretyckes, how moche theyr workes prevaile their wordes.' This ... shewethe playnly to be two maner of heresies; the one to be of perverse teachynge, and the tother of naughty lyfe: of whiche this later is worse and more peryllouse. The whiche raygneth nowe in the churche in pristes not lyvynge pristly but secularly, to the utter and miserable distruction of the churche.[14]

Had the clergy intrigued to teach false doctrine, the detrimental effect would not have been as great as that of the heresy of their "lyvynge secularly," which, according to Colet, extinguished charity in the church and turned the whole community from its saving tasks.

The solution proposed in the 1512 sermon was quite compatible with the recommendation set in Colet's first set of lectures. The laity can be

---

[13]CONV, p. 297.

[14]CONV, pp. 298-99.

reclaimed for righteousness, as can the church itself, if the clergy only return to their pristine goodness. Colet concluded that the clergy could not expect to restore their hold on the loyalties, affections, and obedience of the laity unless they improved their hold on the spirituality of their profession.[15] This is translated in the "reformation" sermon into an appeal to traditional prohibitions.

> The waye whereby the churche may be reformed into better facion is not for to make newe lawes . . . there is no faute but that [the] fathers have provyded very good remedies for hit. There are no trespaces, but that there be lawes against them in the body of Canon lawe. Therefore, hit is no nede that newe lawes and constitutions be made, but that those that are made all redye be kepte. Wherefore in this your assemble let those lawes that are made be called before you and rehersed: those lawes, I say, that restrayne vice, and those that furder virtue.[16]

Colet rooted his remedies in the long struggle of his ancestors for self-reform. He found provisions for the strict examination of ordinands as well as legislation against profiteering. Clauses that secured greater selectivity in the choice of priests, forbade absenteeism, safeguarded promotion according to merit, and detailed procedures for the election of bishops assured that reformation need not rely upon "newe lawes." The tradition of self-reform, however, also provided for provincial councils and reform convocations to monitor the improvement of church life. The prospect of orderly reformation was, for Colet, as much a part of the church's destiny as it had been a part of its history. This was possible because virtue and righteousness not only had been given honored places in Christian soteriology but also had been recognized, with special reference to clerical comportment, as the cornerstones of ecclesiology and church reform.

The reformation of Colet's "reformation" sermon was modeled on countless efforts of reforming councils from the provincial gatherings ordered by Gregory VII to the Lateran just then (1511) called by Julius to enforce clerical discipline and to remove abuses. Colet, in other words,

---

[15]EER-a, p. 228.

[16]CONV, pp. 299-300.

modeled conservatively and with familiar clay. He passed unfavorably on the clergy's oppression of the laity but he also warned that the laity must not ill treat or abandon their clergy. He was acquainted with previous heretical assaults on clerical malfeasance, but too much can be made of this. Colet was not a Lollard, a disciple of John Wyclif; and Professor Rupp illegitimately infers from the few and random notes on Colet in Foxe's martyrology that "Lollards were to be seen, nodding or exchanging patronizing glances during his sermons." Colet's anticlericalism, if it was anticlericalism, was of a different order from the popular hostility against the clergy that had seeped into the tissue of fifteenth-century English (and European) Catholicism.[17] Colet believed simply that the chasm between the high standards of spiritual order shaped in the apostolic church and the prevailing standards of behavior in late medieval churches could be narrowed, if not also bridged, without resort to secession and separatism. He understood, perhaps naively, that the problem itself was not complex. Conformity with the world threatened the extinction of charity within the church. The task, which he undertook long before his 1512 sermon, was to restore the church's appreciation of righteousness as the matrix of order, both in terms of the church's structure and in terms of the *ordo salutis*. Colet believed that he could find no better persons to validate his task and to assist him in its completion than St. Paul and the pseudo-Dionysius.

St. Paul and Divus Dionysius: Church Reform and Church Authority

St. Paul was always at the center of Colet's thoughts. The apostle's opinions were authoritative above all others. However many times he

---

[17]Cf. E. Gordon Rupp, *Studies in the Making of the English Protestant Tradition* (Cambridge, 1949), p. 17. Foxe associated Colet's name with certain Lollard martyrs—one (Thomas Geffrey) was said to have commended Colet's preaching and another (John Lambert) was alleged to have paid him a vague compliment. See *The Acts and Monuments of John Foxe*, ed. Stephen Reed Cattley, 8 vols. (London, 1837-41), 4:229-30; and 5:217. But Colet's name in Foxe's records suggests no affinity between his opinions and the opinions of those hounded by the authorities in his time. Colet certainly would not have condoned the antisacramentalism with which Geffrey was charged. Rupp's inferences, however, are more moderate than certain other evaluations of Colet's orthodoxy. See, in this connection, Karl Bauer, "John Colet und Erasmus von Rotterdam," *Archive für Reformationsgeschichte*, Erganzungsband 5 (1929): 175; and Leland Miles, "Protestant Colet and Catholic More," *Anglican Theological Review* 33 (1951): 42.

read the letter to the Roman church, Colet repeatedly found himself in "a fruitful and pleasant field," filled with timely ideas and instructions.[18] That letter especially defined the task of every church official as the promotion of goodwill and the maintenance of charity in the church community.[19] Elsewhere, however, St. Paul also suggested, at least to Colet, that the reiteration and protection of doctrine were largely the affairs of catechists but that the apostolic commission was to perfect believers "in action, namely in virtue."[20] To the early Christian communities, placed as jewels in an alien Roman setting and divided between Judaizers and antinomians, St. Paul recommended patience, tolerance, and mutual love. Colet may have found the circumstances to which the apostle addressed himself somewhat analogous to those of his own time, but he most certainly found the character of the letters pertinent to his own undertaking.

The teaching of the gospels had long been reconstructed for devotional purposes, but, as Beryl Smalley observed, the Pauline epistles were customarily "resigned to the theologians." Too little is presently known of fifteenth-century exegesis to trace with assurance the persistence of this custom, which was certainly prevalent earlier, but one can still assume that Colet's attitude toward St. Paul represents a point of departure.[21] Lefèvre, Erasmus, and Luther after Colet turned to the Pauline corpus for direction for the life and faith of their churches. Colet, however, did more than rescue the apostle from the prison of medieval speculative and dialectical theology. He steadfastly refused to distinguish St. Paul's message from his personality. Nothing, according to Colet, was

---

[18]EER-b, pp. 190, 197.

[19]EER-b, p. 204: "Sic conatus est bonus apostolus bonum bono elicere, et suo bono aliorum malum vincere. Quem nos omnes debemus imitari, sicut ille Christum, et ante omnia servare in nobismet ipsis, quisque in se et omnes in societate et ecclesia Christiana, quod ab aliis quaerimus; amorem videlicet mutuum et charitatem, quae satis magna et accumulata esse non potest."

[20]EEC, p. 183.

[21]See Jean Baruzi, "Les Diverses interprétations de Saint Paul au seizième siècle," *Revue de théologie et de philosophie* 17 (1929): 81-102; Donald J. Parsons, "John Colet's Stature as Exegete," *Anglican Theological Review* 40 (1958): 36-42; and Beryl Smalley, *The Study of the Bible in the Middle Ages* (Notre Dame, Indiana, 1964), pp. 76-77, 363.

farther from his protagonist's intention and character than the formulation of creed or the arbitration of doctrinal uniformity. Colet sketched St. Paul's chief concerns as the solidarity of the young churches as well as their moral witness, and he orchestrated St. Paul's rebukes and indulgences so that all appeared to have been said and done for the improvement of the church community.[22] Colet admired the apostle's delicate diplomacy, for there the message and personality merged, turning every effort toward the propagation of righteousness and church harmony. St. Paul was *"consideratissimus,"* and his legacy to the Catholic reform, just as his contribution to earliest Christianity, was admonition and confirmation.[23] "By 'calling you to mind,' Paul is not teaching unknown things but reminding you of what you already know."[24]

When, in his commentary on St. Paul's epistles, Jacques Lefèvre d'Étaples suggested that "Paul is only an instrument," he meant that the letters were divinely inspired and that their truths were therefore timeless.[25] Colet's emphasis was discernibly different. His St. Paul was much more a man of method than a man of miracles. The timely truths in the apostle's correspondence were, for Colet, inextricably bound with the author's consciousness of his mission and with his personality. The apostle's message was his exemplary leadership of the church, that is, his prudent acknowledgment of human weakness and his compelling argument for righteousness. Colet understood that admonition and confirmation took flesh in St. Paul's career, in his display of sensitivity and

---

[22]See, for example, EEC, pp. 164-65, 223-24.

[23]EER-a, p. 207.

[24]EER-b, p. 222: " '[I]n memoriam vos reducens.' Quod denotat, non docens ignota, sed admonens scita. Et hoc consonum est ei quod dixit in prima epistola, id est, in prima parte hujus epistolae: 'Desidero enim videre vos, ut aliquid impartiar vobis gratiae spiritalis ad confirmandos vos.' Quod denotat: satis docti estis; sed forsan egetis fraterna admonitione et confirmatione."

[25]*The Prefatory Epistles of Jacques Lefevre d'Etaples and Related Texts*, ed., Eugene F. Rice, Jr. (New York and London, 1972), p. 297 (epistle 96): "At vero qui mundanum forte attendent artificem, immo qui Paulum ipsum qui iam supra mundum est, quasi hae epistolae sint eius opus et non superioris energiae in eo divinitus operatae, suo sensu ad lecturam accedentes, parum fructus inde sunt suscepturi. . . . Nam Paulus solum instrumentum est."

sensibility as much as in the propositions about holiness that had been derived from his letters.[26]

Colet's insistence on the unity of personality and message, and derivatively on the timeliness more than the timelessness of St. Paul's truths, yields more than just another aspect of Colet's identification of reform with righteousness. He accented *"le côte humain du livre divin,"* and thereby he introduced, or at least endorsed, a fresh approach to the sacred texts. In order to retrieve information about St. Paul's statesmanship, the letters would have to be read as "state documents." Extra-canonical sources, never before matched with biblical materials, would have to be employed to illumine the situations in which the saintly diplomat found himself. An historical, as opposed to an exclusively "doctrinal" approach to the Pauline corpus marks Colet as a man of the nascent English renaissance.[27]

Colet incorporated history into hermeneutics, but this was not unprecedented. Nearly fifty years before Colet's lectures, Lorenzo Valla practiced philological surgery on the New Testament: Valla used the text to challenge its own popularly accepted history. This brand of "biblical humanism," however, was foreign to Colet, whose only purpose was to reanimate through his lectures the admirable standards for behavior that the apostle set forth in word and deed. He was at one with Valla in his avoidance of the scholarly custom of accumulating bundles of authorities to prove the historically uninterrupted propriety of a given scriptural interpretation and in his delight in unraveling the circumstances that surrounded and prompted the biblical admonitions and exhortations. Unlike Valla, who has been called "instinctively aggressive" toward the Vulgate[28] and unlike Erasmus, who made so bold as to correct Jerome's Latin, Colet was comparatively semiservile to the text. His inquiries were

---

[26]EEC, pp. 182, 195-96, 268.

[27]See EER-a, pp. 199-200; EER-b, pp. 200-201, 222-26. Also consult Humbert, *Les origines de la théologie moderne,* p. 136; Richard McKeon, "Renaissance and Method in Philosophy," *Studies in the History of Ideas,* 3 vols. (New York, 1918-35), 3: 43-49, 94-95; and P. Albert Duhamel, "The Oxford Lectures of John Colet: An Essay in Defining the English Renaissance," *Journal of the History of Ideas* 14 (1953): 506-10.

[28]Salvatore Garofalo, "Gli umanisti italiani del secolo XV e la Bibbia," *Biblica* 27 (1946): 350-52.

philologically unsophisticated and restricted to topics that were deemed practical. This is to say that Colet's desire to find a model for righteous leadership in the church drove him to the front ranks of the new renaissance hermeneutics. Historical truth was not an end in itself, but a means to promote righteousness. The same can be said with respect to Colet's appreciation for the whole of scripture.

Although Colet warned his good friend Erasmus about the hazards of allegorical exegesis, he failed to follow his own advice.[29] His interest in the personalities behind the texts led him to explore the nature and intention of biblical allegories and led him also to some allegorizing of his own design.[30] The figurative meanings encased in the creation narrative proved to Colet that Moses, like St. Paul, was a consummate diplomat as well as an educator. The "holy fictions" of Moses were devised to promote piety. Consequently, while Colet's interpretations of Genesis embraced several incomplete schemes, foremost among them was a relatively simplistic but practical exegesis of the meaning of the sabbath for contemporary church life.[31] His understanding of the creation narrative was riveted to no master plan of the universe. It did not occur to him, as it did to Pico della Mirandola, to decode sublime mysteries. In Colet's hands, the creation story became a thinly disguised textbook for ethics.[32]

---

[29]Clericus, *Opera Omnia*, 5:1291-92.

[30]See EER-a, pp. 224-25; EEC, p. 237; EER-b, pp. 214-215; and SAC, p. 64. These relatively few outbursts of enthusiasm for typological exegesis are supplemented by Colet's sustained allegories in his remarks on Genesis, *Scripta Joannis Colet, professoris theologiae, decani Sancti Pauli London: in principium Genesios*, in *Opuscula quaedam theologica*, pp. 167-82. On Colet's allegories, see Friedrich Dannenberg, *Das Erbe Platons in England bis zur Bildung Lylys* (Berlin, 1932), pp. 62-63; and Ernest William Hunt, *Dean Colet and His Theology* (London, 1956), pp. 89-98. Here I use "allegory" in the general sense suggested by Jean Pepin, *Mythe et allégorie* (Paris, 1958), p. 248: "Cette distinction entre un sen apparent, que ne dépasse pas le lecteur banal, et un sens profond auquel accèdent les doctes, voilà l'exacte définition de l'allégorie, dans quelque milieu que l'on en use."

[31]*In principium Genesios*, pp. 178-80.

[32]Pico was probably responsible for Colet's initiative *In principium Genesios* (pp. 170-71). See Pico's own commentary, *Heptaplus*, in *Opera omnia*, I (Hildesheim, 1969), pp. 1-62; and translated by Jessie Brewer McGaw (*Heptaplus* [New York, 1977]). Also consult Avery Dulles, *Princeps Concordiae: Pico della Mirandola and the Scholastic Tradition* (Cambridge, Mass., 1941), pp. 76-104. Later in his life Colet expressed considerable doubt about the good sense of Reuchlin's commentaries, which were demonstrably

Notwithstanding his claim that the dutiful exegete must cherish consistency, Colet's own exegesis of Genesis is filled with contradictions and with clumsy transitions from metaphysics to natural science. By comparison, Pico's *Heptaplus* is much more orderly. What unifies Colet's otherwise awkward effort is the profile of Moses as a moral legislator for an uninstructed people (*"rudi genti"*). Colet wanted primarily to retrieve the practical wisdom shrouded by that ancient compulsion, which had apparently seized both Moses and St. Paul, to accommodate inferior intellects. Although he cautioned that the principle of accommodation or condescension could be overused, his caveat hardly prevented him from harvesting practical meanings from stories of all kinds. He left to more restless imaginations whatever esoteric wisdom could be wrung from canonical sagas and parables, but he turned those same stories to the service of righteousness and to the reformation of church life.[33] Thus, while examining the statesmanship of patriarch and apostle, at the heart of which he placed the principle of accommodation, Colet engaged in some delicate diplomacy of his own. He broadened the meaning of the "literal sense" so that inquiry might be made with respect to the meaning of metaphors without departing from the "letter" of scripture, now defined as the hortatory and pedagogical objective of the authors. With one hand, Colet upheld the manifold levels of scriptural meaning. With the other, he domesticated the allegories of Moses and of St. Paul so that they might promote the reform of church life.

---

inspired by Pico (Allen, 2: 599), but Colet's own commentary on 1 Corinthians betrays his early fascination with the Florentine humanist (EEC, pp. 253-54).

[33]*In principium Genesios*, pp. 173, 177. Also see Michael Murrin, *The Veil of Allegory* (Chicago, 1969), pp. 6-11, 70, 120-21, 168. Renaissance allegory coaxed the intelligent reader to penetrate behind the literary veil to the secrets masked by it. When the Renaissance interpreter approached an allegory, he would disregard the "distressingly simple" and distill the profound genius of the text. Murrin asserts that a kind of logos-principle governed the allegorist's enterprise such that the same truth was thought to have inspired both creative and interpretive allegorization. If, however, allegorization ceases to be inspired by a cosmic or psychic truth and is inclined toward and governed by the meager understanding of the common reader, allegory, according to Murrin, became oratory. Despite Colet's use of the term "poet" to refer to Moses, Colet actually understood Moses as an orator. Despite Pico's mention of Moses's egalitarianism and popularity, Pico frankly appreciated the Genesis narrative as poetry that preserves truth for only the few, special readers, well schooled in its mysteries.

Colet's position on St. Paul was founded on his conviction that accommodation was not simply a pedagogical tactic but was actually the bedrock of the apostle's ministry and self-consciousness. Popular ignorance was a factor for Moses, but it appeared to Colet to be less a factor for St. Paul. The earliest Christian communities were endangered by pride, so "among the Corinthians who thought much of themselves, of their knowledge, and of their talents, St. Paul humbled himself even as he proclaimed Christ." This was not, however, a purely political maneuver; it was a gesture that, for Colet, surpassed all others in importance inasmuch as it exemplified the reformation of church life desired by the apostle and by Colet himself. Colet understood that the mysteries of salvation belonged to the humble, to God's faithful servants who live by the spirit. Faith and righteousness, identified here with the spiritual life, possess the secrets of God's new dispensation precisely because they are those secrets. Colet trumpeted the availability of this knowledge to anyone who climbed from the "valley of worldliness and despair"; but he believed that he was only drawing the inescapable conclusions from the Pauline admonitions and confirmations in which accommodation, as the foundation of the apostle's life and theology, guaranteed the triumph of humility and spirituality over worldly conformity. Before they communicated the lessons that they derived from God, St. Paul, "his disciple Dionysius the Areopagite, and several others" took the greatest care that they might seem to be devoid of worldly wisdom.[34] This had great bearing at a time in which competing explanations pretended to unlock divine mysteries, and competition and boasting presumably poisoned the churches, such as the one at Corinth. But it had greater bearing still as the central part of the lesson that the apostle learned about righteousness and about the prospect of its healthy effect upon the harmony and spirituality of the church.[35]

Colet's pairing of St. Paul with the pseudo-Dionysius has always surprised his readers. Many persons assume, as did Luther, that the two early Christian authors were worlds apart.[36] Moreover, Colet's friend

---

[34]EEC, pp. 171-77.

[35]EEC, p. 182.

[36]"De captivitate Babylonica ecclesiae," *D. Martin Luthers Werke* (Weimar, 1888), 6:562, lines 9-12: "[E]tiam perniciossimus est [Dionysius], plus platonisans quam Christianisans. . . . Paulum potius audiamus."

William Grocyn, following a course taken by Lorenzo Valla, all but discredited the pseudo-Dionysius's apostolicity.[37] For Colet, however, there was nothing "pseudo" about St. Paul's alleged protégé for whom he reserved a special place in his developing ecclesiology. According to Colet, "*divus* Dionysius" was chiefly responsible for the orderly succession of ceremonies and sacerdotal responsibilities and, therefore, in some part, responsible for the maintenance of order and of a fraternal spirit in the church. Jews took great care to safeguard their traditions against the nearly imperceptible erosion that culture worked upon religious practices and loyalties; but Christians, in their worldliness, seemed to Colet to contribute to the deterioration of church order. He stated that, were it not for the foresight of "*divus* Dionysius," who set down the details of sacramental observances, Christendom would have been unable to recapture its heritage.[38]

The pseudo-Dionysius not only furnished descriptions of imitable early Christian practices but also supplied a rationale that became the mainstay of Colet's appeal for righteousness and reformation. Colet needed more than a pattern of duties and privileges reconstructed from early Christian literature. He was impressed with the reasons that the pseudo-Dionysius offered for emphasizing the clergy's preeminent position in church life, and he spent considerable energy, probably after he exchanged his Oxford lectern for a London pulpit or perhaps in anticipation of his resettlement, adapting the *Hierarchies* to his own purposes.

The pseudo-Dionysius's *Hierarchies* are ostensibly concerned with the structure of creation, each order of which participates in the diffusion of light to the order immediately below it and participates, in decreasing measure, in the life-giving power of God. God communicates himself through intermediaries who assimilate those below them into their own holiness, and in the case of the ecclesiastical hierarchs, who initiate them sacramentally into the mysteries of the hierarchical pageant and therefore into the mysteries of divine life. Colet, as if he were recoiling from the sumptuous metaphysics of his mentor, understood that mediation

---

[37]See Seebohm, pp. 90-93; and Roberto Weiss, *Humanism in England During the Fifteenth Century*, 2nd ed. (Oxford, 1957), pp. 173-74.

[38]EER-b, pp. 197-98; EEC, p. 171; PSD, pp. 176, 202-204, 210-11, 236-38, 254-55.

was the propagation of righteousness. He interpreted the soteriological reasons for church order and for the ecclesiastical hierarchy that stabilized it, all the while agreeing with the pseudo-Dionysius, though from a different perspective, that precise notions of church structure and practice were absolutely crucial in the return of creation to God. According to Colet's interpretation, the self-disclosure of divine reality in the structure of the cosmos and the church was of less importance than the church's role in restructuring human experience. He accepted the pseudo-Dionysius's assistance and authority in delineating that role as it pertained to the clergy.

The priest was believed to be *"medius inter Deum et hominem,"* an ambassador charged with reducing creation, or that part of it over which his church offices give him power, to its proper order.[39] The envoy's conduct must be exemplary. Colet contended that among this caste divinely set aside to represent and to spread order, there could be no indifference to the most minute details of desirable behavior. God's holiness must be so predominant and profoundly communicated in the lives of church leaders that it could shine forth and attract others to righteousness without diminishing its store.[40] The lowest orders of angels transfer their spirituality to the ranks of clergy "so that they (the clergy) may be made completely spiritual and spiritualize each churchman beneath them according to his capacity."[41]

It must be noted that spiritualization in this usage had many meanings for Colet, as it must have had for the pseudo-Dionysius. Catechumens had to be instructed, penitents cleansed, energumens exorcised, and apostates recaptured for the faith.[42] The clergy were responsible for the

---

[39]SAC, pp. 81-82, 90-91.

[40]EER-b, pp. 187-88; EEC, p. 250; PSD, pp. 206-207, 222; SAC, p. 35.

[41]PSD, pp. 175-76: "Ultimi angeli pontifices nostros et antistites exagitant, extenuantque sursum in spiritum, ut toti scilicet spiritales fiant: ut deinceps alios sub se homines, quemque pro capacitate sua, spiritificent: ut ex hominibus (quoad fieri possit) in Christo quarta hierarchia sit bene spiritalis, qui aliquando veri spiritus erunt et angeli, spiritificatione eorum a Deo in Christo, per angelos et angelicos homines continuata." *Pontifex* in Colet's passages refers not to the papacy in particular but to all bishops. Colet's own position on papal power closely approximated positions held by episcopal enemies of papal monarchy. See PSD, p. 220.

[42]PSD, pp. 248-50.

sacraments and the sacraments for the believer's transformation and *"assimilatio Deo."* All this, however, constituted, in Colet's understanding, only the bare outlines of the "paternal administration and spiritual regeneration" assigned to the clergy, who must be present as models of and guides to the level of righteousness required of God's elect. The clergy were the "living stones," piled hierarchically one upon the others, but all of them formed, in Colet's abstracts, a phalanx for the work of regeneration.[43] Taken in its many parts, that work represented spiritualization and, at its best, conditioned the spirituality of the whole church.

Colet often spoke of the supremacy of the clergy's responsibility to wed the church to Christ. The priest's consecration was a spiritual matrimony of sorts, and it represented the betrothal of the whole church. Colet utilized ideas scattered in the pseudo-Dionysius's *Hierarchies* to formulate and emphasize each priest's obligations to assemble the entire church and to make it worthy of a conjugal relationship with Christ.[44] This rather ambitious commission was composed of three related chores. First, the clergy must prepare and purify lesser members of the church. To this end, Christ instituted and the pseudo-Dionysius preserved the order of the sacraments suitable to direct the clergy to encourage hope, fidelity, and righteousness in the church.[45] Second, the clergy must administer the church and maintain its structural orderliness. As authorities in the spiritual estate, as Christ's brides and stewards, they must watch over his estate until he reclaims his property.[46] Finally, the clergy must keep vigil over their own behavior. The marriage of the whole church to Christ was proleptically present in the marital relationship contracted in the sacrament of ordination and sustained by the fidelity and righteousness of Christ's brides, the clergy.[47] Whether Colet translated the sacerdotal obligations as those of an intermediary, a paternal administrator, or a faithful and busy wife, the elements of his ecclesiology remain constant. And foremost among them was the notion that the

---

[43]PSD, p. 182.

[44]SAC, pp. 35-41.

[45]SAC, pp. 84-85.

[46]SAC, pp. 68-70.

[47]SAC, pp. 39-40.

clergy's righteousness was absolutely necessary for the saving role of the church. It should surprise no one, therefore, that Colet's reformation began with this idea and that he was ultimately reluctant to proceed with any restructuring of the church, its sacraments, or its doctrines.

After considering the controversies that convulsed sixteenth-century European Christianity one has the impression that Colet's call for reform was extremely limited and perhaps reactionary. Given the background of his ideas, particularly in the pseudo-Dionysius's schematization of the origins of the church and of the mediational nature of its ministry, Colet can hardly be expected to have overlooked the justification afforded there for the hierarchical disposition of authority in the late medieval church. Moreover, his esteem for "*divus* Dionysius" stands in marked contrast to later reformers' exclusive reliance upon scripture, or more precisely upon their respective interpretations of scripture. But the fact that Colet considered the mediational role of the ministry as provisional is of tremendous significance. The chief objective of the church was its dissolution and not the perpetuation of its privileges and customs.

Colet nowhere developed systematically his vision of the dissolution of church authority, but he cultivated a certain nostalgia for the simplicity and purity of the earliest Christian communities, awaiting the end of time. More to the point, however, he looked ahead to the time at which the harmony of the church would be perfected, a time foreshadowed in the celebration of the Lord's Supper. The communication of Christ's nature transforms the laity and creates in the church unity where there had been multiplicity. This "*sacramentum conjuncti et unitatis*" is, for Colet, the culmination of the priest's marriage to Christ; but, somewhat paradoxically, it also strips the celebrant of his sacerdotal distinction. Colet alleged that in the transformation signified by communion, all communicants become priests and sacerdotal prerogatives within the church disappear. The church that would be thoroughly prepared for its acceptance by God was a quite different phenomenon from the one that presented itself for acceptance to men.[48]

---

[48]SAC, p. 71: "[N]am est sacerdotis sacerdotium propagare: nihil enim munus et officium cujusque, nisi propagatio ejusdem, et qui se sacrificavit Deo efficere ut secum alii consacraficent, ut tota ecclesia sit sacerdotium consacrificans justitiam, id est, quisque in ea se justum, vivam hostiam, offerat Deo." Also see SAC, p. 93; and EEC, pp. 237, 242-43.

The minimal resemblance between Colet's vision and the ideal of priesthood of all believers, which animated first Lutheran and, later, Anabaptist protests, should not lead anyone to forge some connection between the Englishman's speculation and continental agitation. Colet's editorial about this possible application of the pseudo-Dionysius's *Hierarchies* to a theology of the sacraments and to church polity is nonetheless noteworthy. But more significant for any comparison between Colet's Catholic reform and the more outspoken reformers of the next decades is Colet's unrelenting identification of righteousness with humility. He shared with those reformers, whom, had he lived, he would surely have opposed, a general dissatisfaction with the worldliness of the clergy and with the dilation of ecclesiastical jurisdiction. As brides of Christ, his clergy ideally were humble servants of, but not the purveyors of, righteousness. "All officers in Christianity are ministers but not masters of the church."[49] Furthermore, they have, according to Colet, only the powers to ascertain and interpret divine judgment; they are not in possession of the authority to influence, to suspend, or to commute the verdicts of heaven. Therefore, it would be preposterous to think that church leaders could market indulgences and compel divine compliance with the terms of their purchase. Customarily popes assigned great importance to the "keys passage" in Matthew 16, where the power to bind and loose was given to Peter by Jesus, but Colet considered their interpolations invalid. "So that bishops may not presume too much," he urged, "it must be noted that men do not break the bonds of sin; nor do they have the power of binding and loosing anything. In fact, only God binds and looses."[50] Whatever is

---

[49]EEC, p. 183: "Magistratus in Christianitate omnes non magistri sed ministri sunt ecclesiae. Ministrorum vero est sedulo agere, et laudem non ab hominibus, sed a Deo solo expectare; item non hic, sed post hanc vitam: agnoscere etiam non valere se in ministerio viribus suis, sed facultate a Deo accepta: ideo homines non in suis ministris, sed in Deo solo gloriari oportere."

[50]PSD, pp. 264-65: "Quia est valde annotandum, ut pontifices non insolescant, non esse hominum remittere peccatorum vincula; nec ad eos pertinet potestas solvendi et lignandi quicquam. Solvit enim et ligat solus Deus, et apud se in caelo solvit et ligat omnia. Qui primi sunt in ecclesia, sicuti sunt pontifices, quod illic ligatum et solutum est accipiunt ex revelatione, et acceptum denunciat, et verbis divinam mentem exsequuntur, non propriam. . . . Relaxant et retrahunt, solvunt et ligant homines, non ex fide Deo, quae ligata sunt in caelis, sed quae ipsi volunt, unde omnia disturbantur in terris. Non sunt

done in the church is simply a sign of what has been done in heaven.[51]

The church's conformity with the world was a source of vexation and great frustration for Colet. While the hierarchical framework retained its proper shape, it had lost its purpose, its spirituality, and its legitimacy.

> The whole institution of the church struggles by purgation, illumination, and perfection of its members in Christ for man's steadfast simplicity, wise order, and perfect goodness, after the fashion of the angels' virtues. All this is done so that above the chaos of confusion and worldliness, a bright order of men, simple and perfect in God, may come into existence—a city set on a hill; a light of the world and salt of earth. Such would shine with faith, hope, and charity beneath Christ, its sun, and would illumine and vivify the world. But alas, I grieve, for smoke and horrid darkness from the valley of benighted men has climbed thickly upward for so long that the light of that city is all but extinguished.[52]

Colet's rather purple prose notwithstanding, his perception of the problem that prompted both his "rediscovery" of St. Paul and his adaptation of the pseudo-Dionysius's *Hierarchies* is quite a bit more clear and somewhat more radical than many of his better known contemporaries. He turned to St. Paul for a model for church leadership. To the pseudo-Dionysius he owed his appreciation for the alignment of church offices and for the importance of sacramental rites. Colet, however, backed away from the pseudo-Dionysius's seductive yet suspect preoccupation with

---

executores voluntatis Dei, sed actores propriae. Non testificant quid Deus vult, quod facere debent (nam eorum officium nihil aliud est quam testificatio voluntatis Dei), sed quod ipsi appetunt, demonstrant."

[51]PSD, p. 258: "Omnis nostra actio hic in ecclesia est significatio eorum quae fiunt in caelis. Nam in fide fundamur et credimus ita esse in caelis ut in terris agimus, divinarum rerum dispensationem imitantes."

[52]PSD, p. 248: "Ita tota ecclesiastica institutio, purgatione illuminatione et perfectione in Christo, molitur hominum constantem simplicitatem, et sapientem ordinem, et perfectam bonitatem, ad clarum illud exemplar angelorum; ut super chaos confusionis et mundi, aliquorum hominum in Deo simplicium et perfectorum luculentus ordo extet, quae sit civitas in monte posita, quae sit lux mundi et sal terrae; quae fide, spe et charitate sub sole Christo resplendens, illuminet et vivificet mundum. Sed, proh dolor, fumus et caligo tetra ex valle hominum tenebrosorum tanta jam dudum et tam spissa spiravit sursum, ut civitatis lumen fere obruit. . . . In quo mundo, quod impressit, sigillum Christi turbulenta collisione hominum in tanta rerum confusione oblitteratum est prope et deletum."

esoteric wisdom. To be sure, the sacraments shrouded mysteries from the uninitiated, and part of the sacerdotal obligation was disclosure. But the church's righteousness and spirituality remained uppermost in Colet's considerations. This was not meant to vitiate the great value of the church's intelligence, yet Colet's treatment of the pseudo-Dionysius's *Ecclesiastical Hierarchy* is most memorable for its author's every effort to squeeze practical, moral insight from its metaphysics. At one point in his text, he can almost be heard praying, in the same breath, that bishops better learn God's mysteries and diligently appoint ethical men to the priesthood.[53]

John Colet's "New City of God"

The present appeal of Colet's vision of "the city set upon a hill," the church as a *"nova Dei civitas,"*[54] is less enhanced by his many metaphors than by its natural fit with his soteriology. In his lectures and his abstracts, Colet's analysis of personal spirituality and righteousness led directly to his formulation of an ecclesiology and his sponsorship of church reform. He often spoke of the church as a circle delimited by the Holy Spirit. As boundary or circumference, the Spirit marked off the church from the rest of the world, but the Holy Spirit also permeated the area enclosed within the circumference. There the Spirit bound Christians to one another in mutual affection and service. Without this binding, all the good associated with personal holiness would have come undone, because only a unified church and its members can be "collected" back to God. The maintenance of harmony in the church, therefore, could be said to have been the most important aspect of Colet's description of the regenerative work of the Holy Spirit.[55]

Colet considered it axiomatic that human nature accounted for the nearly irresistible centrifugal force in the church circle. Even more than

---

[53]PSD, p. 227: "Discant igitur pontifices mysteria Dei, et dignos ad sacra sacerdotes promoveant, ne longa indignitate digna ultio provocetur tandem in nos Dei; qui pro sua maxima pietate faciat nos dignos mysteriis suis."

[54]EER-b, p. 176.

[55]See EER-b, p. 187; EER-a, pp. 263-64; PSD, p. 192; EEC, pp. 162, 246-49; and SAC, p. 94.

[56]EEC, pp. 230, 239.

the unwanted intrusion of temporal powers, churchmen's thirsts for private advantage spelled disaster for church harmony and unity.[56] The Holy Spirit, however, achieved what neither law nor gospel, neither doctrine nor decree, could accomplish, the submission of private interest to the common good.[57] In collaboration with human will, in personal regeneration, the Spirit thaws what had been frozen to the possibility of "socialization," and it secures ecclesiastical solidarity against self-will and worldliness.[58]

Colet suggested that the Holy Spirit, taming human nature, worked commonality of aspiration and purpose among individual Christians and, therefore, complete sympathy in the church.

> There is one spirit in all; all are in the one spirit which is of Christ. What is in the lowest member is in all members. Thus there is common feeling, common grief, and common joy. Where the spirit grieves or rejoices, it does so everywhere.... Even when the occasion for grief is not shared, the feeling is shared by virtue of the spiritual unity. In the spirit, all are one in God who is fully present to all who are one so that they may be united to him in common feeling, wisdom, will, desires, and actions.[59]

The Holy Spirit establishes a hidden empire (*latens imperium*) in which sympathy among citizens is stronger than the fellow feeling that often unites members of the same family.[60]

> Although members are diverse in form, in strengths, and in offices, all parts cohere, strive together for unity, and assiduously aid one another because of a certain conciliating nature and life which has proceeded from the head into all the members and joints of the body. As a result, there exists no plurality, but a unity composed of many

---

[57]EEC, p. 234.

[58]EER-a, p. 226; EER-b, p. 154.

[59]CORP, p. 194: "Tam est spiritus unus qui est in omnibus; tam sunt omnes in spiritu uno qui est Christi. Quod est infimo membro, id idem est in omnibus. Hinc est quod sensus dolorque communis est, communeque gaudium. Atque ubi spiritus dolet, ubique dolet; ubi gaudet, simul ubique gaudet: id est, facit dolere et gaudere ... et ubi non est communis lesio, est tamen ex unitate spiritus communis sensus; quia spiritu omnia unum sunt in Deo, qui adest totus omnibus, in se unus, et omnia in se uniantur, sensu, sapientia, voluntate, studiis, actionibusque communibus."

[60]CORP, pp. 187-88; EEC, pp. 221-22.

parts in which there is no private affair and no care for private advantage but a marvelous desire for the commonality, the unity, and the health of the whole body instinctually shared by all.[61]

Church harmony depends, for Colet, less on the imitation of certain virtues and the collective assent to doctrines than on the cardinal principle that self-will and private interests be replaced by a spiritual disposition toward the well-being of the community. This did not mean that one had to relinquish the satisfactions of this life. What is evident, however, is Colet's desire to remove conditions that contributed to dissension in the church and that jeopardized the constant practice of charity and righteousness.

Colet pondered, for example, the antinomy between charity and litigation, and he concluded that every legal contest was underwritten by covetuousness and that covetuousness could not but extinguish the light of Christian love (*"obnigratur candor charitatis"*). Colet forbade Christians to take their complaints to the world's courts. He believed that ecclesiastical arbitration of inescapable rivalries would be sufficient, but he hoped that the contentious spirit that prompted litigation would soon take its leave of the church. "The way to conserve what one has been given," Colet argued, "undoubtedly ought to be identical to the way it was obtained: through love of God and neighbor . . . true piety . . . endurance of evils, and eagerness always to do good for all men."[62]

Although Colet admitted the need "to conserve what has been given," he also permitted himself an outburst against the church's obsession with property. His direct assault on "the law of *meum et tuum*" raised an issue,

---

[61]EER-b, p. 184: "Quae quanquam multae, variae et diversae sunt, tum forma, tum viribus, tum officiis; tamen certe natura et vita conciliante, a corporis capite in omnia membra et artus profecta, omnes partes ita inter se coherent et ad unum constudent, et pro viribus mutuo tam se inter se sedulo coadjuvant, operis ultro citroque collatis, ut in toto non plures, sed ex pluribus partibus unum quidam totum confectum extet, in quibus nulla privata sit ratio, nulla proprii commodi cura, sed ubique et ob omnibus, tacita docente natura, communitatis et unitatis ac totius corporis salutis mirum studium."

[62]EEC, p. 186: "In qua proculdubio eadem debet esse ratio conservandi quae data fuerint quondam, quae fuerit comperandi. Amor Dei et proximi, desiderium coelestium, contemptus mundanorum, vera pietas, religio, charitas, benignitas erga homines, simplicitas, patientia, tollerantia malorum, studium semper bene faciendi vel omnibus hominibus, ut in constanti bono malum vincant." Also note EEC, pp. 189-90.

however, that even he was unprepared to settle.[63] Had Colet desired the alienation of all private properties in the church, he might have hoisted Gratian's recommendation, *"clericis omnia communia esse debent,"* from the canon law[64] and have given it a prominent place in his "reformation" sermon, or perhaps he would have attempted an extension of the monastic ideal. But Colet was no more interested in a radical restructuring of church custom than he was in a reformulation of doctrine. He related the evils of property to those of covetuousness and dissension, demonstrating again that at the heart of his reform program, the ideals of personal righteousness and church harmony regulated the flow of his reformist sympathies. Let the church have its property and let the clergy have their tithes; let them only refrain from quarreling about such things.[65] At best, Colet would have agreed with Aquinas that "in common" refers to the use and not to the ownership of property.[66] That is, one must be prepared charitably to share what one possesses. The real problem was not property but rather the malevolent disposition that made property the object of contention and made churchmen disputatious tax collectors and litigants.

Charity and righteousness were of greater significance than any structural modification that Colet could have stipulated because simultaneously and inseparably they assured personal holiness and ecclesiastical harmony. Both human will and the church were "instruments" of the Holy Spirit, whose signature is scrawled across the parchments of Colet's *ordo salutis* and ecclesiology. Church unity was fashioned by the Holy Spirit and maintained by souls conspiring together (*"ab animis in unum conspirantibus"*) righteously to serve one another and God.[67]

"The establishment and stability of Christ's church is the end of Christianity," Colet reasoned; therefore, only what contributes to the stability and growth of the church was lawful for the Christian.[68] Precise

---

[63]EER-a, pp. 259-60.

[64]*Concordia discordantium canonum,* 2, causa 12, q. 1, c. 9.

[65]EER-b, p. 218: "Verum haec non scribo quod nolim ecclesiam habere possessiones; aut sacerdotes decimas et oblationes; sed ut de hujusmodi nullo modo contendant."

[66]*Summa theologiae,* 2a 2ae, 66, 2.

[67]EEC, p. 254.

[68]EEC, p. 232: "Finis Christianitatis auctio et stabilitas ecclesiae est Christi. . . . Statue

standards for conduct were forgotten. "What is abstractly and *per se* lawful is not necessarily lawful for all, everywhere, and at all times. . . . We ought to consider not so much what we can do as what is conducive to society to union and to peace."[69] What was both soteriologically and ecclesiologically unexceptionable, for Colet and, he trusted, for St. Paul, was the precept that Christians must be bound by the Holy Spirit to wish for the common weal and to certify that aspiration with righteous action.[70] This precept was universal, as the Christian's quest for salvation was universal, but Colet specified that each member of the church must ascertain the limits of his abilities and obedience, "for each knows himself best."[71]

Colet appeared mindful of the dreadful personal and institutional consequences that could follow an attempt to enforce strict standards for doctrinal and behavioral conformity. Church leaders counsel and advise. To preserve church solidarity and stability, the strong tolerate the short-comings of weaker Christians, just as Moses and St. Paul recognized limitations even as they fueled the desire for perfection. If it be said that the church would not exist without some conformity and compulsion, then these putatively necessary conditions would fall to the province of the Holy Spirit, whose prerogatives, according to Colet, were to loose the grip of self-will and worldliness and to bind the Christian to the church. As we have learned, however, this was not, in the strictest sense, compulsion. Colet provided that the Spirit, and grace generally, operated "*suaviter*" upon nature, collaborating with human will while furnishing it with new strengths. He noted then that levels of accommodation, whether in the development of spirituality, in the manipulation of biblical language, or in the exercise of leadership, corresponded to various stages in the propagation of righteousness ("*in propagatione justitiae*"), which was

---

ergo tecum hoc tantummodo licere, tantumque te hoc posse, quod prosit ecclesiae incremento et stabilitati illius."

[69]EER-b, p. 209: "Quod enim per se et simpliciter licit, idem apud omnes et omni loco et tempore non licet. Quod autem ex fide et amore et fraterna pietate fit, id nusquam nunquamque potest esse non licitum. Non tam quid nos possumus, quam quid conducat societati, unioni, et paci spectandum est."

[70]EER-a, p. 243.

[71]EEC, pp. 212-15.

the common objective of the divine, the apostolic, and the sacerdotal projects in the church and in the world.

The preceding explorations have made one thing apparent: Colet's soteriology constituted the backbone of his conceptions of church stability and service. His every affirmation of church life, prescription for church leadership, and recommendation for church reform had wholly determinate soteriological overtones. Reformation begins with the elimination of clerical scandals. Addressing those clergy assembled in 1512 to renew the attack on doctrinal irregularities, Colet put his own pleading against the clergy's injustices and worldliness as if he were but a pious layman. "Unto you we loke as unto markes of our direction. In you and in your lyfe we desyre to rede, as in lyvely bokes, howe and after what facion we may lyve . . . . You spirituall phisitions, fyrst taste you this medicine of purgation of maners, and then after offre us the same to taste."[72] Righteousness, spirituality, and therefore reform could neither be legislated *per modum auctoritatis* nor effected by more efficient courts and treasuries, and so Colet saw no great advantage in the redistribution of authority and resources within the church. Reform in and of the church required moral reeducation. As Walter Schirmer succinctly noted in his discussion of *englische Frühhumanismus*, John Colet advanced the noble equation of piety with reformation ("*Frömmigkeit wird Reformation*"), an equation that gives the appearance of something simple and self-evident when placed alongside the more complex and doctrinally oriented reformations of the sixteenth century but nevertheless denotes a profound adaptation of Augustine's thoughts on righteousness and reform to the problems of late medieval Christianity.[73]

---

[72]CONV, p. 299.

[73]Walter Schirmer, *Der englische Frühhumanismus* (Leipzig, 1931), pp. 180-81. Also note Piero Rebora, "Aspetti dell'Umanesimo in Inghilterra," *La Rinascita* 2 (1939): 383.

An Augustinian Tradition in the Sixteenth Century

Erasmus, Belles-lettres, and Righteousness

There is no single doctrine or lesson in Colet's Oxford lectures that is astonishingly fresh and seductive, yet Erasmus reported that they were extraordinarily well-attended.[1] The lectures were all but forgotten by English Protestants and Catholics alike until the search for home-grown reformers who might rival Luther gathered momentum among scholars in France and England in the nineteenth century. By then the rising tide of nationalism propelled French and English scholars into their respective archives in search of indigenous reformations. What is most important for my purposes in tracing certain continuities in the ideas of salvation and reform, however, is Erasmus's own attraction to John Colet's lectures and the nature and extent of his intellectual indebtedness to Colet.

The last century of Renaissance and Reformation scholarship has been marked by several discussions of Colet's influence upon Erasmus.

---

[1] Allen, *Opus epistolarum*, 4:515-16, lines 281-90: "Iam reversus ex Italia, relictis parentum aedibus Oxoniae maluit agere. Illic publice et gratis Paulinas Epistolas omnes enarravit. Hic hominem nosse coepi, nam eodem tum me deus nescio quis adegerat; natus tum erat annos ferme triginta, me minor duobus aut tribus mensibus. In theologica professione nullum omnino gradum nec assequutus erat nec ambierat: tamen nullus erat illic doctor vel theologiae vel juris, nullus abbas aut alioqui dignitate praeditus quin illum audiret, etiam allatis codicibus; sive hoc laudis debetur Coleti autoritati, sive illorum studio quos non puduerit senes a juvene, doctores a non doctore discere."

Albert Hyma charged that such influence was a modern fiction imposed upon medieval fact that, properly mined, would disclose the *Devotio Moderna*'s virtual hegemony over Erasmus's formative years. Others have not denied but rather have narrowly restricted Colet's reach. For Ivan Pusino, Lamberto Borghi, and Raymond Marcel, Colet was simply the go-between who introduced Erasmus to the Florentine Neoplatonists. An alliance of sorts had formed among these American, German, Italian, and French scholars in order to counter the extravagant assertions of Colet's significance for Erasmus that first appeared in Victorian literature.[2] Frederic Seebohm, the enterprising English scholar, and his disciple, Joseph H. Lupton, pioneered the recovery and study of Colet's lectures and miscellaneous treatises and also tended to overstate Colet's influence. They conveyed the general impression that Colet had disabused Erasmus of his interests in scholasticism and had instilled in his new friend a wholesome and sobering perspective on current ecclesiastical improprieties. According to Seebohm and Lupton, Colet made Erasmus a religious reformer. Erasmus then exported Colet's "Oxford Reformation" to partisans of both Catholic and Protestant Reformations on the continent who were inclined to modify rather than to undermine venerable religious practices and institutions.[3] Adaptations of the Victorian understanding have become commonplace in later European and American studies. They far outnumber the few papers written to dispute the central role in Erasmus's biography assigned to Colet by Seebohm's

---

[2]See Albert Hyma, "Erasmus and the Oxford Reformers (1493-1503)," *Nederlansch archief voor kerkgeschiedenis* 25 (1939): 68-92, 97-134; reprinted, in part, in Albert Hyma, *Renaissance to Reformation* (Grand Rapids, Michigan, 1951), pp. 209-49. Also note Ivan Pusino, "Der Einfluss Picos auf Erasmus," *Zeitschrift für Kirchengeschichte* 46 (1928): 75-96; Lamberto Borghi, *Umanesimo e concezione religiosa in Erasmo di Rotterdam*, Studi di lettere storiae filosophia, vol. 7 (Florence, 1935); and Raymond Marcel, "Les 'découvertes' d'Erasmus en Angleterre," *Bibliothèque d'humanisme et Renaissance* 14 (1952): 117-23.

[3]Frederic Seebohm chronicled the "fellow work" of Colet, Erasmus, and Thomas More and he argued that their shared concern for religious renewal justified his own choice of title, *The Oxford Reformation* (3rd ed., London, 1887). In addition to editing all and translating most of Colet's surviving work, Joseph Lupton completed two monographs: *The Influence of Dean Colet upon the Reformation of the English Church* (London, 1893), and *A Life of Dean Colet*, 2nd ed. (London, 1909).

and Lupton's heirs, and they are probably responsible for today's under-graduate appreciation of the friendship between Colet and Erasmus.[4]

Erasmus first met Colet in 1499. There is no foolproof way to determine whether he came to England that year to pass a summer vacation or to further his studies. Erasmus's enthusiasm for Paris, where he had been studying theology for nearly four years and privately instruct-ing other visitors in composition and rhetoric, had certainly waned, but it would be unreasonable to suspect, as did Helmuth Exner, that Erasmus was undergoing something of an identity crisis when he crossed the Channel.[5] One of his pupils in Paris, William Blount, invited Erasmus to London, probably for only a short holiday. But when King Henry VII forbade vessels from carrying unlicensed passengers to the continent, Erasmus may have found himself unexpectedly detained. It is likely that only then he decided to visit Oxford, where, after the customary exchange of flattering letters, he fell into frequent conversations with John Colet. Notwithstanding their disagreements on certain issues of exegesis, Eras-mus confessed that nothing gave him greater delight "than debating daily the meaning of scripture either face to face or through correspondence."[6] He had long craved leisure and learned company, and during his few months at Oxford, he enjoyed both.

More than a decade before he first sailed for England, Erasmus entered the Augustinian monastery at Steyn. Although he later alleged that his guardians had pressured him, at the time he was probably

---

[4]See, for example, Augustin Renaudet, *Préréforme et humanisme à Paris pendant les premiers guerres d'Italie* (1494-1517) (Paris, 1916), pp. 387-88; Karl Bauer, "John Colet und Erasmus von Rotterdam," *Archiv für Reformationsgeschichte*, Erganzungsband 5 (1929): 155-87; John A. R. Marriott, *The Life of John Colet* (London, 1933); Helmuth Exner, *Der Einfluss des Erasmus auf die englische Bildungsidee* (Berlin, 1939), pp. 104-105; P. Albert Duhamel, "The Oxford Lectures of John Colet: An Essay in Defining the English Renaissance," *Journal of the History of Ideas* 14 (1953): 493-510; and E. Harris Harbison, *The Christian Scholar in the Age of the Reformation* (New York, 1956), pp. 70-78.

[5]Consult Exner, pp. 15-16.

[6]Allen, *Opus epistolarum*, 1: 249, lines 112-13: "Interim nihil mihi possit esse dulcius quam (ita ut coepimus) quotidie vel coram vel per epistolas de sacris litteris inter nos conflictari." Also see James D. Tracy, *Erasmus, The Growth of a Mind* (Geneva, 1972), pp. 83-84.

compelled more by the leisure and literary culture afforded by the cloister. Beyond Steyn life was, at best, tumultuous and uncertain. Wealth, worldly pleasures, and secular status and honors were short-lived, as he wrote in his *De contemptu mundi*, and an unhealthy amount of time and worry must be spent protecting them from the envy and perfidy of friends and enemies alike. His *Oratio de pace et discordia*, also written at Steyn, laments humankind's failure to live in keeping with its natural nobility. In contrast with other animals, humans have no horns, claws, sharp teeth, or poisonous venom, but they have a much milder nature inclined toward peaceful social intercourse. Unlike the most ferocious beasts, however, humans cannot maintain harmony within their own species.[7] The *Oratio*'s arguments were heavily weighted with commonplaces from the literature of antiquity and virtually devoid of biblical and patristic material. Astonishingly, the *De contemptu* was similarly imbalanced. Erasmus, when we first hear from him, has apparently mistaken the pursuit of secular learning and the conveniences permitted him in his retreat for the religious life and devotion customarily expected of medieval monks.

One looks in vain in Erasmus's *De contemptu mundi* for an inventory of traditional ascetic virtues. Tranquillity, peace of mind, and freedom have supplanted obedience, poverty, celibacy, and constant prayer. Still, this is not a sign of irreligion. Erasmus broadly conceived of religion as the pursuit of knowledge in God's service, and he yearned for worthy men to join him in a community of scholars sheltered from worldly concerns by Steyn and by other monasteries in the Low Countries. The first eleven chapters of the *De contemptu* were addressed to a prospect, perhaps his good friend William Herman, to encourage him to abandon "the world" and find sanctuary and the pleasures of peaceful study at Steyn. His correspondence is full of exhortations to study and fellowship. But years passed and the "community" did not materialize. Erasmus appears disturbed and somewhat desperate when replies to his letters were not immediately forthcoming. Late in 1489, a controversy over the merits of Lorenzo Valla seems to have left his most cherished friendship (with Cornelius Gerard) in shambles. Furthermore, as he bitterly complained

---

[7]See J. Clericus, ed., *Opera omnia Des. Erasmi Roterodami*, 10 vols. (Leiden, 1703-1706), 8:547.

decades later, his superiors grew intolerant of his pursuits and they possibly tried to suppress the interests that originally led their young colleague to Steyn. Erasmus probably schemed with Herman to leave and to continue their studies in a friendlier setting; but, as luck would have it, another friend procured an appointment for him in 1493 as secretary to the Bishop of Cambrai, and suddenly Erasmus was gone.[8]

Erasmus hoped to accompany his bishop to Italy, but the trip was canceled. He traveled instead through Burgundy until, in 1495, he was dispatched by his patron to study theology in Paris. Erasmus's work at the university with the Scotists required special exertions toward which he was disinclined, and he gravitated more toward a group of humanists who were not associated with the theology faculty. With them, his sense of the independent instructional value of classical literature deepened, but he carefully phrased a letter home, prominently and piously displaying religious motives and criteria that purportedly governed his selection and pursuit of studies.[9]

Among Parisian humanists, Erasmus's favorite was Robert Gaguin, who, as sometime dean of the Faculty of Canon Law, as versifier on sacred subjects, as ardent Francophile and historian of France, and as frequent ambassador for the crown, seemed to have skilfully juggled religious and secular interests.[10] The few letters from this period that survive indicate that Erasmus found his older colleague a generous host and sympathetic critic. To Gaguin he submitted a draft of the first of his four projected books against barbarous schoolmasters who disdained the literature and erudition of antiquity and who paraded their obscurantism beneath banners of piety and simplicity (*"rusticitas"*). Gaguin suggested that

---

[8]See Hermans' letter to Erasmus in Allen, *Opus epistolarum*, 1:129-30. Also see the most recent edition of the *De contemptu mundi* in *Opera omnia Desiderii Erasmi Roterodami*, 5.1 (Amsterdam, 1977). For reports of Erasmus's early friendships and for penetrating studies of his early disappointments, see C. Reedijk, *The Poems of Erasmus* (Leiden, 1956) and Albert Rabil, Jr., *Erasmus and the New Testament: The Mind of a Christian Humanist* (San Antonio, Texas, 1972).

[9]Allen, *Opus epistolarum*, 1:161-64.

[10]See Louis Thuasne, ed., *Epistole et orationes Gaguini*, 2 vols. (Paris, 1903). Also consult Franco Simone, "Robert Gaguin ed il suo cenacolo umanistico," *Aevum* 13 (1939), pp. 424-25, 433-34.

Erasmus break the lengthy speeches with dialogue, but he was clearly impressed with his visitor's achievement, the *Liber apologeticus*, later revised and published as the *Antibarbari*.

> Now although I myself simply hold the impudence of these people in contempt, nevertheless I do not disapprove of the campaign you have launched against them. They should be assailed with every kind of weapon: you have accumulated these with discretion and can shoot them skilfully and brandish them most fiercely, and it would be superfluous for me to give you any advice on their use and wrong of me to seek to take anything away from or add anything to a work you have already finished. You outline your scheme most succinctly, clearly classify the divisions of your subject-matter, and conduct the argument with great skill. Your arrangement is well planned, you adorn your theme attractively, and you have something of Carneades' vigor in controversy.[11]

This is not the review of an unconventional work. The apology's theme, form, and substance, if not its vigor, were immediately familiar to Gaguin. Actually the project's *Grundschema* had been formulated by Erasmus well before he left the monastery, and its sentiments, images, and sources circulated freely among Dutch humanists as they apparently did among Parisian humanists. Still, the *Liber apologeticus* demonstrates the imaginative leadership that Erasmus gave to the causes so dear to humanists in Holland and Paris, namely, the legitimation of classical literature, the appreciation of classical style, and the value for Christian education of humanistic learning.[12]

---

[11]Allen, *Opus epistolarum*, 1:153, lines 24-31: "Et horum proculdubio impudentiam tametsi contemptui habeo, non improbo tamen propositam tibi in eos miliciam. Feriendi sunt omni genere telorum qu[a]e scite admodum congesta iacularis probe et acerrime torques. In qua re supervacuum quidem consilium tibi meum accederet, qui absoluto iam operi nec detrahere nec adiicere quicquam recte possum. Rem enim conceptam multa brevitate proponis, partiris luculenter et summo pertractas ingenio. Apte componis, ornas venuste; nec deest tibi Carneadis vehemens disputatio."

[12]Albert Hyma printed the first draft of the apology in his *The Youth of Erasmus* (Ann Arbor, Michigan, 1930), pp. 242-331. My citations refer to Kazimierz Kumaniecki's edition in *Opera omnia Desiderii Erasmi Roterodami* I.1 (Amsterdam, 1969), pp. 35-138. On the nature and extent of Erasmus's changes, see Rudolf Pfeiffer, "Die Wandlungen der 'Antibarbari,' " in *Ausgewählte Schriften* (Munich, 1960), pp. 188-207 (reprinted from *Gedenkschrift zum 400. Todestag des Erasmus von Rotterdam* [Basel, 1936], pp. 50-68)

As early as 1489 Erasmus was collecting materials for his *Liber apologeticus*. Cornelius Gerard advised him of the suitability of Jerome's arguments and images, and the fourth-century scholar figured prominently in Erasmus's defense of antiquity.[13] While Jerome had contested the charges of erudite pagans (Celsus, Porphyry, and Julian) that Christianity was a hazardous amalgam of simplicity and superstition, Erasmus borrowed from Jerome in order to controvert the simplicity and superstition of churchmen who campaigned against classical literature and to emphasize the compatibility of piety with classical thought and style. Gerard himself collaborated with Erasmus on a poem against barbarism, and originally he was assigned the role of spokesman in the apology.[14] But before Erasmus handed the manuscript to Gaguin, Gerard had been replaced by Jacob Batt, the friend who obtained Erasmus's appointment with the Bishop of Cambrai. The bishop was reportedly a *"vir litterarum amicus,"* so Erasmus may have been given some time to develop the apology's arguments between 1492 and 1495, but Erasmus is known to have complained of *"immodicae occupationes"* that would have prevented extensive revision.[15] The topic itself never ceased to interest him. Theology, according to the *Liber apologeticus*, was principally the knowl-

---

and James D. Tracy, "The 1489 and 1494 Versions of Erasmus' Antibarbarorum Liber," *Humanistica Lovaniensia* 20 (1971), pp. 81-120; and the introduction to M. M. Phillips's edition and translation of the *Antibarbari* in volume 23 of *The Collected Works of Erasmus* (Toronto, 1978).

[13]The late date assigned to Erasmus's request for counsel and assistance in accumulating sources, 1494, has been convincingly challenged by Vittorio de Caprariis, "Per la datazione di due lettere di Erasmo," *Rivista storica Italiana* 64 (1952): 222-31. Erasmus employed Jerome extensively in his apology ("cum tantum ac talem habeamus autorem, exoriere tu nobis et nescio quod glossema e tuis barbaris autoribus contra liberalem eruditionem obiicies." [Kumaniecki, p. 113, lines 14-16]), and the letter requesting aid (Allen, *Opus epistolarum*, 1:136, lines 14-19) was copied along with the *Liber apologeticus* in the ninth volume of Erasmus's 1516 edition of the *Opera Hieronymi*. For Gerard's early (1489) prodding with respect to Jerome's suitability, see Allen, *Opus epistolarum*, 1:103, line 20.

[14]"Apologia Erasmi et Cornelii sub dialogo lamentabili auumpta adversos barbaros, qui veterem eloquentiam contemnunt, et doctam poesim derident," printed in Reedijk, *The Poems of Erasmus*, pp. 162-70.

[15]Allen, *Opus epistolarum*, 1:144, lines 5-8. Herman, not Erasmus, wrote of the Bishop's support of scholarship. See Allen, 1:138, lines 73-74.

edge of arguments of ecclesiastical writers employed persuasively to discredit pious obscurantism and to acquit classical literature and antiquity of charges registered against them in the name of Christianity.[16] This understanding matured even after the text was given to Gaguin, but the apology by common consent belongs to the period before Erasmus first encountered John Colet, who modified his appreciation of religious life and thought.

Silvano Cavazza's is, to my knowledge, the lone dissenting voice. He believes that at Oxford Erasmus shook free from the convictions (*"pregiudizi religiosi"*), which held him until 1499, and abandoned late medieval humanism's thinly disguised diffidence toward antiquity. Building upon Ernst-Wilhelm Kohls's tremendously ambitious reading of the apology's speculative theology, Cavazza reconstructs from the *Liber apologeticus* a "religious program" that, he asserts, could not conceivably have flowered in the wilderness of Dutch and Parisian humanism.[17] Elsewhere I have contested Cavazza's claims on textual grounds. Here it is sufficient to add that notions that Cavazza considers too fresh for Erasmus's Paris years and therefore attributable to Colet were included in Erasmus's 1496 letter to his bishop.[18] On only one matter did the *Liber apologeticus* point forward to Erasmus's friendship with Colet and to the *Enchiridion* that Erasmus wrote upon his return from England.

---

[16]See my "The Disputed Date of Erasmus's *Liber Apologeticus*," *Medievalia et Humanistica*, n.s. 10 (1981): 148-51; but also consult Marjorie O'Rourke Boyle, *Christening Pagan Mysteries* (Toronto, 1981), pp. 3-25.

[17]Silvano Cavazza, "la cronologia degli 'Antibarbari' e le origini del pensiero religioso di Erasmo," *Rinascimento* 15 (1975): 141-79; Ernst-Wilhelm Kohls, *Die Theologie des Erasmus*, 2 vols. (Basel, 1966), especially 1:67-68.

[18]Allen, *Opus epistolarum*, 1:163, lines 82-96: "Contra fere fit ut ii quibus felicius ingenium contigit, nescio quo pacto aut ad glorie anane studium male erecti sunt aut ad lasciviam pejus proclives; ceterum a Christiane religionis pietate simplicitateque abhorrent. Quare recentioribus his poetis, atque adeo Christianis, subirasci mecum interdum soleo, quod in deligendis sibi archetypis Catullum, Tibullum, Propercium, Nasonem quam divum Ambrosium, quam Paulum Nolanum, quam Prudentium, quam Juvencum, quam Mosen, quam David, quam Salomonem sibi proponere malint, tanquam non sponte sint Christiani. Sed reprimam me ne plus satis, praesertim in amasios quondam meos, ut isti me insimulant. Equidem cum meo Gaguino libens sentio, qui ecclesiasticas quoque materias vernaculis opibus splendescere posse putat, modo pura adsit oratio. Neque improvaberim Aegyptiam adhiberi supellectilem; verum totam Aegyptum transferri non placet."

The apology reflects Erasmus's earliest fascination with Augustine. Before Erasmus met Colet and in this treatise against barbarous Christians, Jerome was still *"primus doctorum."*[19] Appropriately the surviving text of the apology had been copied on empty sheets in Erasmus's edition of Jerome's works. From those works Erasmus derived much, if not most, of his knowledge of many other church fathers named in the *Liber apologeticus.* Augustine, however, was the exception. Earlier Erasmus paired Augustine with Jerome in order to make their friendship a model for those which he hoped to cultivate from Steyn, but the early correspondence gives no indication that Erasmus was familiar with any of Augustine's treatises.[20] In the apology Erasmus commented on stylistic shortcomings that may have encouraged him to keep his distance from the venerable theologian and might have been cause for him to exclude Augustine altogether from the pages of the apology had Augustine not furnished invaluable corroboration for one of his most cherished hypotheses: the whole earth is the Lord's, so even the gentiles provided useful knowledge and crafts that Christians could guiltlessly commandeer.

Only in 1494 did Erasmus discover Augustine's usefulness. While serving the Bishop of Cambrai but just before he arrived in Paris, Erasmus chanced upon a copy of the *De doctrina Christiana* in Groenendal. Twenty years later his excitement was still fresh in the memory of William of Louvain to whom we owe the only account of Erasmus's discovery. Erasmus himself insisted later that during his adolescence he had always preferred Augustine to Jerome, but his recollection was probably prejudiced by the popularity of Augustine at the time he made his statement (1518). Religious controversy had by then eclipsed cultural revival and Augustine had outdistanced Jerome in terms of their importance to those from whom Erasmus would have had to seek advantage. At the age of twenty-six, Erasmus had enthusiasm primarily, if not exclusively, for Augustine's *De doctrina* because its favorable verdict on non-Christian learning could easily be incorporated into his *Liber*

---

[19]Kumaniecki, p. 130, line 4. Also see p. 127, lines 8-10.

[20]See, for example, Allen, *Opus epistolarum*, 1:99, lines 89-101; 104, lines 10-21; and 125, lines 83-87.

apologeticus.[21]

Augustine was not master of style, as was Jerome, but he was master of argument. Erasmus, however, had ears only for arguments that were to his liking. Augustine captivated his young Dutch reader with his persuasive case for ancient learning, but Augustine's more vigorous remarks on the captivity of human will were scarcely, if at all, heard. Erasmus had maintained in his early correspondence that God sold his grace at the price of human effort. Apparently deaf to Augustine's much more nuanced appreciation of grace, will, and human righteousness, he reconstructed the same Pelagian position in his *Liber apologeticus.*[22] Before his first trip to England and his visits with Colet, Erasmus saw no need to ascertain the truth or even the meaning of the complex claims of his predecessors. Theology was simply the shrewd employment of arguments accumulated from ecclesiastical writers to establish precedents for his own support of classical learning. There is no sign that Augustine led Erasmus beyond this understanding. The *Liber apologeticus* contained few notions that were more than vague reminiscences of patristic theology. That is to say that, notwithstanding his affections for Jerome and Augustine, Erasmus did not aspire to a leading part in a patristic revival. His church fathers were enlisted to campaign for a revival of classical learning; and while this may have heralded a new epoch in the history of humanism, as Karl Meissinger has suggested, Erasmus had not yet

---

[21]Charles Béné exaggerated the importance of Erasmus's "discovery" at Groenendal, suggesting that Erasmus's loyalty had decisively shifted from Jerome to Augustine. Béné is too credulous with respect to Erasmus's 1518 recollections (Allen, *Opus epistolarum,* 3:337, lines 263-67). See Béné, *Erasme et Saint Augustin* (Geneva, 1969), pp. 63-66. William of Louvain's report of Erasmus's reading of the *De doctrina* appears in his letter to Martin Lipsius. The account is reprinted in Allen, *Opus epistolarum,* 1:590.

[22]Kumaniecki, p. 133, lines 24-27. The same position appears in Erasmus's 1488 letter to Servatius Rogerus (Allen, *Opus epistolarum,* 1:88-89, lines 9-19): "[E]t tu bonae spei columen dormienti tibi haec confecturos deos putas? Num eam legisti fabellam, quae in rustico tuam condemnat incuriam? Nam is cum forte quadrigae suae rotam luto haerere nec a jugalibus evelli posse conspiceret, ipse otiosus in auxilium summos invocasse divos dicitur; quo jam dudum incassum orante [quo nihil exorante] id Apollo e nubibus oraculi reddiderit: si tibi auxilio esse deos cupis, ipse quoque dexteram admoveas necesse est. Haud aliter tu quoque, Servati mi, si tantus te (ut ais) literarum tenet affectus, tua imprimis opera opus est; nec divum nec hominum quemquam profuturum speres, si tibi defueris ipse. Omnia enim dii mortalibus labore vendunt."

grappled with the moral and theological issues that would further transform his belletrism into a more far-reaching concern with the reformation of Christian thought and life.[23]

By 1501, however, Erasmus was busy developing his understandings
of piety and reform along lines suggested by his new friend, John Colet.
That same year, at the request of "a woman of singular piety," he
arranged a series of canons for Christian conduct.[24] Later printed as the
Enchiridion militis Christianae (1503), his composition was intended to
improve the manners of the woman's husband; but the influence of the
manual far surpassed the modest expectations of its solicitor and its
author. The *Enchiridion* survives as Erasmus's most complete expression
of a theology of the Christian life. "May this book not make for theological disputation," he wrote fifteen years after its initial publication, "but
rather for a theological life."[25] Busy laymen would find it impossible to
keep in close touch with the most current theological thinking on the
conduct befitting a Christian, so Erasmus attempted to place a handy
summation at their sides and in their purses, too small to hold the whole
of Aquinas's *Secunda secundae*. Yet, certainly by 1518, Erasmus was also
aware that his manual was more than a simple summation and that it
represented something of a new departure.

> What would be achieved by dealing with those things with which
> everyone deals? Who is not presently busy with theological ques-
> tions? Are the swarms of schoolmen concerned with anything other
> than that? There are nearly as many commentaries on the books of
> *Sentences* as there are theologians. Is there anyone other than those
> who mix commentaries and mix again, in the way of pharmacists,
> repeatedly arranging and rearranging old potions from new, new
> from old, one from many, and many from one? What is to be done so

---

[23]K. A. Meissinger, "Erasmus entdeckt seine Situation: Gedanken über die *Antibarbari*," *Archiv für Reformationsgeschichte* 37 (1940): 196-97.

[24]Consult Otto Schottenloher, "Erasmus, Johann Poppenruyter und die Entstehung
des *Enchiridion militis christiani*," *Archiv für Reformationsgeschichte* 45 (1954): 113-16.

[25]See the prefatory letter to Paul Volz, printed with the 1518 edition of the
Enchiridion and reprinted in *Desiderius Erasmus Roterodamus ausgewählte Werke*, ed.
Hajo Holborn and Annemarie Holborn (Munich, 1933), p. 4, lines 5-6: "Non faciat ad
disputationem theologicam, modo faciat ad vitam theologicam."

that the vast heap of these volumes might teach us to live well: not even an entire lifetime is sufficient to sort them.[26]

Erasmus, then, tried his hand at "applied theology." Selected scriptural principles were carefully fashioned into a *ratio vivendi*. This led Erasmus to relinquish some of the ground gained in his apology. He had discovered a new and fascinating area of research compared to which secular literature was but a *"cibus temporarius,"* a snack or, at best, a light meal next to the boundless manna provided by scriptural study.[27] And when, in the *Enchiridion*, Erasmus applauded the ancients, it was, more often than not, to shame amoral Christians—not to convert them to pagan moral philosophies, but to reconvert them to Christ.

True piety was disclosed in the example set by Jesus, *"in quo omnes insunt beate vivendi rationes."* He died to obtain pardon for humankind so that persons might live as worthily as he had lived. His death was the subject of endless doctrinal speculation, much of which Erasmus had collected in his own treatise on Christ's passion.[28] His life was a simple object of imitation and the true concern of the *Enchiridion*. Erasmus was thinking of this dichotomy when he contended that Jesus purposefully concealed this sublime person (Christ as *"maximus"*) and avidly revealed his virtues (Christ as *"optimus"*). The imitable virtues instruct the faithful, even the theologically unsophisticated, in spiritual and ethical regeneration.

---

[26]Ibid., lines 6-15: "Quorsum autem attinet hoc tractare, quod nemo non tractat? Quis hodie non versatur in quaestionibus theologicis? Aut quid aliud agunt gymnasiorum examina? Tot paene sunt in Sententiarum libros comentarii quot theologorum nomina. Quis summulariorum modus aut numerus aliud ex alio miscentium ac remiscentium et pharmacopolarum ritu ex novis vetera, ex veteribus nova, e pluribus unum, ex uno plura subinde figentium ac refigentium? qui fiet, ut hujusmodi voluminum moles nos ad recte vivendum instituant, quae ne per omnem quidem vitam vacet evolvere?"

[27]*Enchiridion*, in *Ausgewählte Werke*, p. 33, lines 7-10. In search of weapons to vanquish unrighteousness, the Christian may enter foreign arsenals, but Erasmus considered the scriptural stores superior to those in the non-Christian classics of antiquity (*Enchiridion*, p. 35, line 23-p. 38, line 3). Erasmus admired eclectic Christians, notably Pico and Reuchlin. The *Enchiridion*, however, leaves no doubt as to the respective merits of Christian and non-Christian learning.

[28]"Disputatiuncula de taedio, pavore, et tristitia Jesu," in Clericus, *Opera omnia*, 5: 1256-94.

So that you can journey to felicity on a more certain course . . . set your sights on Christ as the only goal of your whole life. Direct all your desires, endeavors, leisure, and business toward him. Think not of Christ as an empty expression but as charity, simplicity, patience, and purity; in brief, as everything he taught.[29]

Christ's life remained in the memory of the medieval world as an epitome of human nobility and a sure example of the righteousness required for salvation. St. Paul's letters, on the other hand, had not been a favorite resource for medieval devotional literature. Scholastic exegesis had its way with the letters, and the apostle's moral theology became little more than a sourcebook for the intricate doctrinal debates that preoccupied theologians. But Colet unmasked St. Paul for Erasmus, who, immediately upon his return from England, started a series of commentaries on the Pauline correspondence. More than a decade later (1511), when Erasmus again contemplated writing on St. Paul, he teased Colet with the thought, "perhaps I shall be so bold as to enter into *your* Paul" ("*Paulum tuum aggredi*").[30] Save for the Paulinism of the *Enchiridion*, Erasmus's first commentaries have not survived; but placed in his manual alongside the familiar lesson of Christ's life, St. Paul became for Erasmus the

---

[29]*Enchiridion*, p. 63, lines 8-13: "Sed ut certiore cursu queas ad felicitatem contendere . . . ut totius vitae tuae Christum velut unicum scopum praefigas, ad quem unum omnia studia, omnes conatus, omne otium ac negotium conferas. Christum vero esse puta non vocem inanem, sed nihil aliud quam caritatem, simplicitatem, patientiam, puritatem, breviter quicquid ille docuit."

[30]Allen, *Opus epistolarum*, 1:466, line 20. Colet's peculiar combination of Pauline theology and Platonic spirituality is discussed by Kurt Schroeder, *Platonismus in der englischen Renaissance vor und bei Thomas Eliot*, pp. 32-35; and Friedrich Dannenberg, *Das Erbe Platons in England bis zur Bildung Lylys*, pp. 77-79. Adaptations somewhat similar to those of Colet are noted in the *Enchiridion* by Alfons Auer, *Die vollkommene Frömmigkeit des Christen nach dem "Enchiridion militis Christiani" des Erasmus von Rotterdam* (Düsseldorf, 1954), pp. 78-84, 94-101; and John B. Payne, "Toward the Hermeneutics of Erasmus," *Scrinium Erasmianum*, ed. J. Coppens, 2 vols. (Leiden, 1969), 2: 17-25. Erasmus might have only intended to suggest that he would follow Colet's more or less historical and, in few places, philological approach to the letters (Duhamel, "The Oxford Lectures of John Colet," pp. 504-506). I argue here, as I have elsewhere, that Erasmus's attraction to Colet's reading of St. Paul and his subsequent deployment of the epistles in the *Enchiridion* were founded upon the concern with righteousness and reformation that Colet and Erasmus shared. See my "John Colet and Erasmus' *Enchiridion*," *Church History* 46 (1977): 296-312.

preeminent theologian of the Christian life: "Do we need a better teacher of religion?"[31]

With abundant citations from St. Paul's letters, Erasmus's handbook for the Christian soldier analyzes the flawed methods used by the church to appease God and to quench the layman's thirst for redemption. Visible forms of worship and punctiliously performed sacrifices were held in high esteem by the apostle's *quondam* opponents but also, it seemed to Erasmus, by the medieval church. Erasmus's own approach to the problem of salvation in an increasingly secular society started with St. Paul's stern disapproval of ceremonialism and then contrasted laws and formulae that inflated the importance of ceremonial observances with the apostle's counsels that prudently emphasized the importance of personal piety. "You may judge your brother by his food, drink, or attire; but St. Paul judges you by your deeds."[32] God is moved by nothing short of a living, spiritual sacrifice; a contrite heart and humble demeanor, in short, "newness of life," count more than a collection of penitential psalms and oblations. Erasmus tenaciously held on to that affirmation as he outlined the distinctions between carnal and spiritual worship of God and between the adoration of Christ in sacramental observances and the imitation of Christ in moral conduct. Both sets of distinctions, the Pauline material deployed to support and elucidate them, and the moral theology that they promote demonstrate the *Enchiridion*'s close affinity with Colet's lectures. Colet and Erasmus shared a desire to reconstruct the late medieval understanding of Christian worship and to underline the significance of the spiritual life, which offers up righteousness as homage to God paid in the currency of a well-lived life among men.

Colet made much of St. Paul's condemnation of those who had trusted in their laws and ceremonies to win God's approval. He announced in his lectures on Paul's letters that ritual was bereft of life-giving power. Only the "law of Christ" generated righteousness and led to new life. In place of a perfunctory performance of sacrifices and ceremonies, St. Paul

---

[31]*Enchiridion*, p. 82, lines 21-22: "Num meliorem religionis magistrum requirimus, praesertim cum huic omnis divina scriptura concinat?"

[32]Ibid., p. 80, lines 32-33: "Tu fratrem in cibo aut potu cultuve judicas. At Paulus te judicat ex factis tuis."

demanded total dedication to the humble virtues exhibited by Christ and an active righteousness that follows from faith. Had Erasmus been attentive to Colet's lectures or had he discussed soteriology and moral theology with Colet during their frequent interviews, he would surely have been exposed to the two themes dear to his English friend. The first secured redemption only for those whose participation in the sacraments was sealed by moral regeneration. Colet asserted that the marrow of Christianity consisted in the quality of life inspired by the traditional ceremonies and not in the ceremonies themselves. Where St. Paul argued that outward circumcision was of no value unless the circumcised obey the law (Romans 2:25-29), Colet interpolated by substituting "baptism and other sacraments" for "circumcision" and "gospel" for "law."

> Baptism and other sacraments are beneficial if you obey the gospel; but if you break the gospel, your baptism is unbaptism. Therefore, if the pagan keeps the upright precepts of the gospel, will not his unbaptism be reputed as baptism? and will you, a Christian by birth and baptism yet a breaker of the gospel, not then be judged by one who, although a pagan, completes the gospel?[33]

The second theme is closely related to the first. Having identified St. Paul's emphasis upon active righteousness, Colet developed his own understanding of those works, inspired by faith and aided by grace, in contradistinction to the unrighteousness of works prescribed by law and performed solely by the believer. The old law that commanded sacrifices from the herds and from the fields prefigured the gospel that demanded spiritual propitiation. The spiritual life was, in Colet's estimation, the highest offering one can make to God. It best prosecutes the penitent's case, far better than ritual oblations. Traces of this, Colet's interpretation of the apostle's moral theology and soteriology, are clearly present in Erasmus's *Enchiridion* where the righteous life is equated with a living, spiritual sacrifice and where the part of man that corresponds to the

---

[33]EER-b, p. 227: "Baptismus et alia sacramenta quidem prosunt, si evangelium observes. Si autem privaricator evangelii sis, baptismus tuus paganismus est. Si igitur paganus justitias evangelii custodiat, nonne paganismus illius in baptismum reputabitur? et judicabit is qui ex natura est paganus, evangelium consummans, te Christianum, qui per carnem et baptismum privaricator es evangelii?"

spiritual world is nothing other than his Christian ethical standards of excellence.[34]

Colet's sense of the persistence of moral theology in the apostle's writing is perhaps his richest intuition. It inclined him toward what Rudolf Padberg, in speaking of Erasmus, has called "humanistic Catholicism."[35] Colet sketched a more recondite interaction between divine and human wills than the schoolmen would have been disposed to tolerate, but he insisted that grace was the foundation of piety. He defined virtue in terms of the Christian's daily struggle for perfection and he saw that struggle as of far greater significance for theology than the slow growth through the centuries in the sophistication and complexity of *scientia divina*. Erasmus extended Colet's sketch of "humanistic Catholicism" into a full-formed moral theology and he drew Colet's understanding of the fellow-work of God and man, as his rightful wage, into the development of his own soteriology in the *Enchiridion* and later in his disputes with Martin Luther.

Padberg's characterization of "humanistic Catholicism" is important because it captures the presuppositions shared by Colet and Erasmus. Although it will be somewhat disconcerting for persons long accustomed to hearing of Erasmus as a "mere moralist" to find him in the *Enchiridion* agreeing with Colet on the priority of grace, that is, the gift of the spirit, the conclusion is inescapable. In the *Liber apologeticus*, Erasmus unabashedly proclaimed that spiritual aid was the divine reward for unaided human effort. The *Enchiridion* only vaguely hints that spiritual blessings were rewards for strenuous effort in studies and moral conduct, but even these ambiguous promises are offset by Erasmus's resolute insistence that "spiritual living" was a divine gift rather than a human achievement. Of course, as a devotional manual replete with maxims, warnings, and encouragements, the *Enchiridion* depicts life as a struggle and urges believers to become worthy of the victory assured by spiritual assistance. Unquestionably, however, the divine spirit is the foundation of piety, and, according to Erasmus, St. Paul correctly reduced soteriologi-

---

[34]*Enchiridion*, p. 67, line 34-p. 68, line 14.

[35]Consult Rudolf Padberg, *Erasmus als Katechet* (Freiburg, 1956), especially pp. 63-64.

cal and ethical issues to the imperative to allot to the spirit sufficient attention and proper respect.[36] For Erasmus, as for Colet, theology followed the apostle's imperative without denying the centrality of the Christian struggle for perfection. Precisely this is at the heart of "humanistic Catholicism." After his visits with Colet, Erasmus was unlikely to repeat his earlier ruling that theology's chief purpose was the vindication of *belles-lettres*.

The idea that grace's priority must be confirmed in moral theology and soteriology without undermining values placed on human industry was not at all foreign to scholasticism. The rise of "humanistic Catholicism" did not occur in isolation from scholastic attempts to place the Christian life in, but not entirely of, the world. It would be more accurate to say that Colet and Erasmus took refuge in a voluntaristic mysticism in response to complex scholastic differentiations between the respective roles of divine and human wills in the economy of redemption. Colet and Erasmus appealed to the principle that animated scholastic soteriology— grace transforms and completes nature—theirs was a lean version of their predecessors' syntheses. Erasmus had become disenchanted with the schoolmen while he studied with the Scotists at the University of Paris. He believed that his teachers were so entangled in their own syllogisms that they could not alert themselves to the desirability of applying their theologies to the genuinely religious needs of Christians. Colet had independently trimmed scholastic soteriology and had returned to a more primitive synergism associated with Augustine's understanding of grace and will but attributed directly to St. Paul's moral theology. Fresh from Paris, Erasmus discovered and adopted this Oxford alternative. When he returned to the continent he made common cause with his

---

[36]*Enchiridion*, p. 52, lines 28-31; p. 69, lines 7-21; p. 72, lines 16-24; p. 81, lines 19-26. Auer, followed by Tracy, put forward a case for the primacy of anthropological concerns in passages such as these. See Auer's *Die vollkommene Frömmigkeit*, pp. 63-79 and Tracy's *Erasmus, The Growth of a Mind*, pp. 104-107. I have argued elsewhere for Ernst-Wilhelm Kohls's convincing qualification of the "anthropologische Grundlegung" of Erasmus's *Enchiridion*. See Kohls's *Die Theologie des Erasmus*, 1: 91-93, my "Colet, Erasmus, and the Practical Spirituality of the Catholic Reformation," *Proceedings of the Second Mid-Atlantic Patristic, Medieval, and Renaissance Conference* (Villanova, 1979), pp. 19-30; and Catherine Jarrott's recent essay, "Erasmus's Annotations and Colet's Commentaries on Paul," *Essays on the Work of Erasmus*, p. 136.

English friend by composing his own "commentary" on the Pauline letters and by setting it in the context of his applied theology, the *Enchiridion*. Later, as we shall see, he recognized his debt to Augustine in a way that Colet himself had not recognized his. But in 1501, Erasmus allowed that his prescriptions for the Christian soldier and for the reform of the church were owed to Colet's recovery of St. Paul.

He repaid Colet many times over. Colet himself was quickly forgotten by his successors yet his aims and interests survived in the immensely popular manual that had been coaxed from Erasmus. Erasmus also wrote a short biography of his friend in 1521, which Martin Tindall translated into English a dozen years later so that Colet "may walk a borde in his own contre, where he may visite his kinffolke, his frends, his familieres, and his scoleres, or rather godsones . . . for all be not yet dede."[37] But Erasmus's greatest service was the preservation of Colet's thought in his *Enchiridion*, not as a system of many parts but as an exhortation reminding its readers of the soteriological significance of moral regeneration.

One such reader was William Tyndale, who, though infatuated with the theology of Luther, balked at the extreme form of the doctrine of saving faith's all-sufficiency. Tyndale's "Parable of the Wicked Mammon" sets forth the theme that recurs throughout his works: faith which justifies must profit one's neighbor or else "faith is but a dream." Salvation is not ultimately contingent upon faith, which may tend toward complacency, but rather salvation rests upon active righteousness and faith active in neighborly love. It has been persuasively argued that Tyndale, who was extraordinarily well-versed in his Erasmus and particularly fond of the *Enchiridion*, inspired Puritan piety, which placed even greater emphasis upon moral consciousness and upon the effects of conversion on conduct. If the *Enchiridion* was rooted in English soil, in John Colet's "humanistic Catholicism" and his conviction that Pauline

---

[37]Quoted from Harleian ms. 6989, in James Kelsey McConica, *English Humanists and Reformation Politics* (Oxford, 1965), pp. 119-20. Tindall's translation has been lost. With respect to the popularity of the *Enchiridion*, see the list of sixteenth-century editions in *Bibliotheca Erasmiana* (Ghent, 1893), pp. 79-82. An English translation is reported for 1518; and, according to Helmuth Exner, England eagerly accepted Erasmus *"als Helfer und Lehrer einer ganz und gar christlichen Frömmigkeit"* (*Der Einfluss des Erasmus*, pp. 104-106).

precepts and practical spirituality plotted identical courses for the life of faith, Erasmus appears to have been responsible for the place of honor in the Tudor reformations that, although generally unacknowledged by his immediate heirs, may now be reserved for Colet and his Oxford lectures.[38]

The fault for Colet's relative anonymity does not lie with Erasmus. He lavished compliments upon his friend from the very first and often within earshot of their mutual friends. Several months after Colet's death, he eulogized the Englishman as "so rare an example of Christian piety and so exceptional a teacher of Christian doctrine."[39] And by "*doctrina*," in this instance, Erasmus certainly meant Colet's understanding of the spiritual life and the importance of moral regeneration for church reform. Martin Luther and, to a considerable extent, William Tyndale understood clerical abuses and immoralities as but symptoms of false doctrine, and theirs were reformations that assuredly associated dissent with disloyalty in the minds of generations of Catholics to come. But another line of thought, one that intersected the more prominent at several places, had been drawn before the outbreak of strictly doctrinal controversies. With Colet and with the Erasmus of the *Enchiridion*, an evangelical revival of sorts had gathered momentum and had concentrated on reconstructing St. Paul's contributions to Christian morality. Later Protestants would turn to St. Paul for authentic doctrine, but these "humanistic Catholics" looked to the apostle to promote a practical spirituality that might transform their lumbering bureaucracy.

"Humanistic Catholicism" and Catholic Reform

Colet's polemical purpose was to rehabilitate the church by reminding his colleagues of the standards for conduct spread throughout St. Paul's correspondence. The violent moralism that erupted intermittently during Colet's lectures coupled with his famous "reformation sermon" of

---

[38]See Leonard J. Tinterud, "A Reappraisal of William Tyndale's Debt to Martin Luther," *Church History* 31 (1962): 41-42.

[39]See Erasmus's letter to John Fisher, Allen, *Opus epistolarum*, 4:94, lines 43-46: "At ego publico nomine non possum non deplorare tam rarum Christianae pietatis exemplar, tam singularem Christianae doctrinae praeconem; privatim autem meo nomine tam constantem amicum tamque incomparabilem patronum."

1512 demonstrably place him in the forefront of early sixteenth-century Catholic reform. Erasmus must have heard him inveigh against clerical impiety during his brief stay in Oxford, and Colet kept his friend informed thereafter about his own troubles with those whom he dared encourage to reform. Like Erasmus, Colet had run afoul of the Scotists, and quite naturally Erasmus sprang to his colleague's defense.[40] And while Erasmus at Steyn was first to arouse official animosity by championing the cause of education, Colet's subsequent founding of St. Paul's School made him reformer *non gratis* in London. In 1512, he told Erasmus a story which must have resurrected the Dutchman's memories of his own travail and of the genesis of the *Liber apologeticus*.

> I have one ridiculous thing to relate to you. I have heard that a certain bishop who is considered one of the more knowledgeable churchmen publicly blasphemed our school. He said that I have established a useless thing; to use his own words, an evil thing, yes, even a house of idolatry. I think that he said this because poets are taught here. Erasmus, I am not so much angered by these words, but rather I laugh heartily at them.[41]

But as much as they shared recourse to humor (Erasmus, however, was far more adept at making the obnoxious appear ludicrous) and as much as they had common likes and dislikes with respect to educational reform (Erasmus, again, had higher ranking and greater tenure as an educational reformer, although he himself scrupulously avoided his turns at the lectern), Colet and Erasmus stand most closely together as "humanistic Catholics" and therefore as reformers of church life and practice.

The close connection between Pauline soteriology and the *desideranda* of church reform distinguishes "humanistic Catholicism" and Catholic Reform, on the one hand, from the more ambitious theological reforms undertaken on the continent in the names of St. Paul and Augustine and, on the other, from the more specific reforms proposed by

---

[40]Allen, *Opus epistolarum*, 1:470, lines 19-25.

[41]Ibid., 1:508, lines 7-13: "Unum tibi significo ridiculum, quendam episcopum (uti acceperam) et eum qui habetur ex sapientioribus, in magno hominum conventu nostram scholam blasphemasse dixisseque me erexisse rem inutilem; imo malam, imo etiam (ut illius verbis utar) domum idolatriae. Quod quidem arbitror eum dixisse, propterea quod illic docentur poetae. Ad ista, Erasme, non irascor, sed rideo valde."

late medieval pontiffs and by the fifth Lateran Council. However many opinions about faith, reason, law, gospel, grace, and human will might be amassed from scholastic treatments of the apostle's letters or framed in opposition to alleged scholastic pelagianisms, the simple mandate of Romans 12:2 captured the imaginations of Colet and Erasmus. The "*noli conformari . . . sed reformari*" passage introduced Colet's famous 1512 "reformation sermon." But more than a decade before that, in his Oxford lectures, he definitely recognized the importance of the passage for the reform of late medieval Christianity.

> [St. Paul] implores all persons to join together, to withdraw from the squalor of this world, and to bind their bodies in obedience to reason and their souls. As material purged and readied, they might then submit themselves to a divine reformation. Thus each person may be siezed by divine grace; and inspired by the divine spirit, he or she may become wholly new and divine. Thereafter a new city of God may be formed and may stand forth on earth among those reformed persons. . . . This is what St. Paul demands, namely that the Romans should be reformed to a new sense of things, that they should make manifest in their actions what God wills and what is good and perfect in God's sight, that is, what pleases God rather than what is pleasing to themselves. They should demonstrate that they are possessed not of self-will but of the divine will . . . so that the church may then be good and perfect.[42]

Erasmus, for his part, adapted the pattern of Colet's interpretation to the message of his own *Enchiridion*: "Dare to fix in your soul the teachings of your religion and to follow your creator's will." Persons engaged in worldly pursuits should not be preoccupied with popular canards and

---

[42]EER-b, pp. 175-76: "[I]deo deinde nunc obsecrat, obtestaturque omnes, ut contrahant se et componant; hoc est, abducant se omnino a sordibus hujus mundi, et corpus astringant in obsequium animae et rationis, et quasi aptam et expurgatam materiam se divinae reformationi subjiciant; ut quisque, divina gratia apprehensus, divinoque spiritu afflatus, totus novus et divinus fiat; utque ex omnibus innovatis nova Dei civitas et coelestis construatur in terris et extet. . . . Id est quod hic Paulus jubet, videlicet ut Romani reformentur in novum sensum rerum et judicum, ut probent et ostendant factis quid Deus velit, quidque bonum et perfectum et Deo est placens, non quid sibi; ut non deinceps nunc propriam, sed divinam in se voluntatem habere ostendant . . . utque tota societas et ecclesia bona et perfecta existat."

vanities (*"Noli in malis conformari huic saeculo"*); they should rather be ever mindful of the apostle's spiritual directive: *"sed reformari in novitate sensu tui, sed probes . . . quae sit voluntas dei."* A few sentences later Erasmus briefly spelled out the implications of this directive for the health and unity of the church.

> Recall how little you merited the beneficence of Christ. He wants you to repay, not him, but your neighbor. Watch for what your neighbor needs and for what you are able to do. Think of this: your neighbor is your brother in God, you are together with him in Christ, a member of the same body, redeemed by the same blood, sharing in the same faith, called into the same grace and toward the happiness of a future life.[43]

Too much stress, according to Erasmus, had been placed upon the worship of saints and the adoration of relics. "You worship saints and delight in touching their relics, but you scorn their true legacy, the example of a pure life. . . . Do you wish to be worthy of Peter and Paul? You will do better to imitate the faith of the one and the charity of the other than to run around Rome ten times."[44]

The *Enchiridion* managed to move beyond its cautious appreciation of some Christian observances as props (*"adminincula pietatis"*) toward an unequivocal condemnation of persons who smugly relied upon them as the surest solutions to the riddle of redemption. Colet showed some greater appreciation for ceremonies that marked the official life of the church. He was not as willing, as often, to hurl invective past the

---

[43]*Enchiridion*, p. 99, lines 10-12; p. 100, lines 1-7: "Aude et tu sectae tuae decreta penitus in animo figere, aude securus ac totus in auctoris tui sententiam pedibus discedere. . . . [T]antum memineris, quo merito tibi quae praestiterit Christus, qui suam in te beneficientiam non in se, sed in proximo voluit retaliari. Tantum vide, quibus egeat ille et quid tu possis. Tantum hoc cogita: Frater est in domino, cohaeres in Christo, ejusdem corporis membrum, eodem redemptus sanguine, fidei communis socius, ad eandem gratiam et felicitatem futurae vitae vocatus."

[44]Ibid., p. 74, lines 20-27: "Veneraris divos, gaudes eorum reliquias contingere. Sed contemnis, quod illi reliquerunt, optimum, puta vitae purae exempla. Nullus cultus gratior Mariae, quam si Mariae humilitatem imiteris. Nulla religio sanctis acceptior magisque propria, quam si virtutem illorum exprimere labores. Vis tibi demereri Petrum aut Paulum? Alterius fidem, alterius imitare caritatem, et plus feceris, quam si decies Romam cursitaris."

criminally negligent prelates and directly at the church's most cherished institutions and practices, which, in Erasmus's judgment, tended to trap the faithful at lower levels of piety than that to which they should aspire. Strictly speaking then, the *Enchiridion* does not echo Colet's lectures. Still, there is no gainsaying that Colet left a lasting mark on Erasmus's religious consciousness and that, under his Oxford friend's influence, Erasmus engaged St. Paul in his efforts to make religious service (*"charitatis officii"*) the essence of religion, the goal of theology, and the impetus for ecclesiastical reform. Although those efforts were as much eclipsed as served by Erasmus's later philological interests, as late as 1523, Wolfgang Capito hailed the then accomplished scholar as the instigator of not only a renaissance of literary culture but also a revival of piety.[45]

"Proponamus Augustinum"

Capito's tribute preceded by one year the onset of Erasmus's active participation in the controversy that has found its way into most general history books. Although he had often been coaxed and collared to write against Martin Luther, it was only in 1524 that Erasmus committed to print one of his several objections to Luther's reformulations of doctrine. Colet had been dead five years, but his influence upon Erasmus reached into the cautious restructuring of St. Paul's understanding of grace and will that appeared in Erasmus's challenge to Luther, the *De libero arbitrio*. The popular misconception that Erasmus wrote as a Pelagian has been painfully slow in dying, partly because it is a product of the romancing that has made of Erasmus a modern rather than a sixteenth-century religious humanist and partly because Erasmus himself let slip a definition of human freedom that apparently defended the will's auto-

---

[45]Allen, *Opus epistolarum*, 5:294, lines 28-30: "Nescio quid homini in mentem venerit ut te, autorem cum renascentium literarum tum redeuntis pietatis, impetendum statueret." Also see Erasmus's letter to Colet, Allen, *Opus epistolarum*, 1:479, lines 81-85: "Atque is [quidam non infimae opinionis] corrugato naso subsannans, 'Si quis' inquit 'velit omnino servire Christo, ingrediatur monasterium ac religionem.' Respondi Paulum in charitatis officiis ponere veram religionem; charitatem autem in hoc esse ut proximis quam maxime prosimus." Consult C. Augustijn, *Erasmus vernieuwer van kerk en theologie* (Baarn, 1967), pp. 53-54, 61-62, and 121-22.

nomy in matters pertaining to salvation.[46] The entire treatise, however, argues a case that is precisely the reverse of what one might reasonably expect on the basis of the ill-contrived definition. The *De libero arbitrio* holds that St. Paul accurately ascribed human righteousness to God's generosity and that the human will's ability to cooperate with divine grace was itself an effect of grace. Had the treatise been written some twenty years earlier, and without the dubious benefit of the terms of debate set by Luther, Erasmus might have simply reiterated the theme of his *Enchiridion*: spiritual living was a divine gift rather than a human achievement, but it was also the freely and righteously willed response to God's love that warmed the soul.[47] But the issue of human righteousness, insofar as its genesis and soteriological significance were concerned, had been advanced in a different way by 1524, and Erasmus adjusted his presentation of the theme he had carried forward from Colet's lectures.

The desired reconciliation between grace and human will had been complicated by the prospect that some unsuspecting theologian might impute merit to human activity were the delicate balance between grace and will tipped ever so slightly toward the latter. Luther realized this and uncompromisingly acclaimed the sovereignty of grace and labored the helplessness of fallen human nature and human will. It had been alleged that some small amount of autonomy existed before God looked favorably upon the sinner and that the exercise of that freedom in the service of virtue was necessary to win divine favor. Luther insisted otherwise. Hardly any autonomy, if it was autonomy at all and not just a dreadful illusion, was too much autonomy.[48]

---

[46]*De libero arbitrio*, in *Ausgewählte Schriften*, vol. 4, ed. Werner Welzig (Darmstadt, 1969), p. 36: "Porro liberum arbitrium hoc loco sentimus vim humanae voluntatis, qua se possit homo applicare ad ea, quae perducunt ad aeternam salutem, aut ab iisdem avertere."

[47]See Ernst-Wilhelm Kohls, "La Position théologique d'Erasme et la tradition dans le *De libero arbitrio*," *Colloquium Erasmianum* (Mons, 1968), pp. 70-71.

[48]This was the theme of Luther's *Disputatio contra scholasticam theologiam, D. M. Luthers Werke. Kritische Gesamtausgabe*, vol. 1 (Weimar, 1883), pp. 224-28. The *Disputatio* concentrated its attack on Gabriel Biel, whom Luther pressed for having followed Ockham's suggestion that some virtue was attainable without prevenient supernatural assistance. On Luther and Ockham, see Reinhard Schwarz, *Fides, Spes, und Caritas beim jungen Luther* (Berlin, 1962), pp. 32-39; and Paul Vignaux, "Sur Luther et Ockham,"

Erasmus's meditation on the will's freedom conceded that every act of the will that appeared worthy of grace was itself suffused by grace. He was as much in earnest as he had been in the *Enchiridion* about the moral value of principles largely independent of the gospel. The ancients whose precepts were so like those of the evangelists "probably possessed wills in some way prone to virtue but their wills were ineffective with respect to salvation unless, through faith, grace was added."[49] Erasmus risked the possibility that some merit might be ascribed along with freedom to virtuous wills, but "merit" and "freedom," as he calculated them, were nothing without grace.

> Diligently hunting for Christ in Paul's letters, blessed Augustine merited finding him. But here we are able to placate those who say that man can do no good which is not owed to God. We may confirm that all our works are owed to God without whom we would be ineffective and that the free will contributes very little. Finally, it is God's gift that we can turn ourselves toward things pertaining to salvation and cooperate with grace. Augustine was more unfavorably disposed toward free will after his controversy with Pelagius than he had been before. But, on the contrary, Luther, previously attributing something to free will, now denies it completely in the heat of his defense.[50]

Franziskanische Studien 32 (1950): 21-30. On Luther and Biel, consult Leif Grane, *Contra Gabrielem: Luthers Auseinandersetzung mit Gabriel Biel in der "Disputatio Contra Scholasticam Theologiam, 1517"* (Gylendal, 1962). On the development of Luther's position, see, inter alia, Heinrich Bornkamm, "Sur Frage der *Justitia Dei* beim jungen Luther," *Archiv für Reformationsgeschichte* 52 (1961): 16-29; 53 (1962): 1-60; and Heiko A. Obermann, " '*Facientibus quod in se est non denegat gratiam*': Robert Holcot, O. P. and the Beginnings of Luther's Theology," *Harvard Theological Review* 55 (1962): 317-42.

[49]*De libero arbitrio*, p. 44: "Et in his probabile est fuisse voluntatem aliquo modo propensam ad honesta, sed inefficacem ad salutem aeternam, nisi per fidem accederet gratia."

[50]Ibid., p. 170: "Divus Augustinus dum sedulo quaerit Christum in Paulinis epistolis, meruit invenire. Hic illos, qui non ferunt quicquam boni hominem posse, quod non debeat deo, sic placare possumus, ut dicamus, nihilo secius totum opus deberi deo, sine quo nihil efficeremus, et quod affert momenti liberum arbitrium, perpusillum esse et hoc ipsum esse divini muneris, ut possimus animum ad ea, quae sunt salutis, afflectere aut gratiae guvepyeiv. Augustinus ex colluctatione cum Pelagio factus est iniquior libero arbitrior, quam fuerat antea. Contra Lutherus ante nonnihil tribuens libero arbitrio huc provectus est calore defensionis, ut in totum tolleret."

The last sentences in this passage are noteworthy, for they clearly contrast Luther's denial of free will with Augustine's more nuanced considerations. And Erasmus earlier pronounced "sufficiently probable" Augustine's opinions framed in opposition to Pelagius.[51]

> Saint Augustine and those who follow him, considering that man's trust in his own powers was a danger to true piety, were inclined, just as St. Paul, to favor grace. Augustine contends that man, fallen into sin, cannot change himself and correct his life and cannot do anything which might lead to salvation unless he is moved by unmerited divine grace to wish for those things which do lead to eternal life. Others call this grace prevenient; Augustine calls it operative grace. Faith which is the door to salvation is an unmerited gift of God. Charity which Augustine calls a cooperative grace is a further gift of the spirit added to faith. Cooperative grace always assists those who struggle until they reach what they desire. Free will and grace work together, but grace is the leader of the venture and not merely associated with it.[52]

Erasmus invoked Augustine again in his *Hyperaspistes*, two books of rambling explanations of the position set forth in the *De libero arbitrio*. Even where scripture appeared to place human will absolutely in divine power, Augustine probed further and rescued human will from utter powerlessness. The hardening of Pharaoh's heart must be attributed to God (*"per justum judicium"*) but also to the unfortunate Pharaoh himself (*"per liberum arbitrium"*).[53] Luther, in Erasmus's estimation, exercised less imagination and less sense in biblical interpretation. He held Luther

---

[51]Ibid., p. 56.

[52]Ibid., pp. 50-52: "Sanctus Augustinus et qui hunc sequuntur, considerantes, quanta sit pernicies verae pietatis hominem fidere suis viribus, propensiores sunt in favorem gratiae, quam ubique Paulus inculcat. Eoque negat hominem obnoxium peccato posse sese reflectere ad vitae correctionem aut quicquam posse facere, quod conferat ad salutem, nisi gratuito dei dono stimuletur divinitus, ut velit ea, quae conducunt ad vitam aeternam; hanc gratiam alii praevenientem vocant, Augustinus operantem. Nam et fides, quae ianua est salutis, gratuitum dei donum est. Huic additam caritatem per uberius donum spiritus appellat gratiam cooperantem, quod semper adsit conantibus, donec assequantur, quod expetunt, sed ita tamen, ut cum simul idem opus operentur liberum arbitrium et gratia, gratia tamen dux sit operis, non comes."

[53]*Hyperaspistes*, in Clericus, *Opera omnia*, 10:1396, D-E.

responsible for introducing the language of determinism into the debate. Although Luther allowed freedom of choice in matters of little consequence, Erasmus saw through this concession, which, for Erasmus, told greatly against the consistency of the reformer's cause. As stated and defended, Luther's principle appeared inflexible: God would not suspend the general operation of his omnipotence. A person could not freely turn toward God's grace or away from sinful habits, but neither could a person choose to kill a capon for the evening meal.[54]

It had appeared to Erasmus that Luther had done away with the assurances in Christian tradition that doctrine need not sacrifice human responsibility to divine sovereignty. Not only the Fathers but the scriptures as well vouchsafed some part for human righteousness in the earliest stages of the redemptive process. If human will's servitude to sin was a captivity so profound that it robbed a person of all freedom, then humanity had been reduced to a collection of puppets. The puppet master retained a sovereignty but at a cost that was, for Erasmus, so extraordinary as to be unthinkable. Erasmus also understood, however, that scripture and tradition were generous with their assurances with respect to the priority of divine grace. This could have meant temporal priority—hence the proliferation of preparatory graces in the theories of the scholastics who attempted to reconcile divine priority with human responsibility. Erasmus agreed that whatever little effort advanced a person toward righteousness and redemptively significant attitudes and actions, such effort was not wanting the grace of God. Grace need not be prevenient to that effort, however, but necessary for it and coefficient with it.

> It is more plausible to acknowledge that the little effort, insufficient of itself, of a man advancing ever so slightly in this affair is not without God's grace. Still, you would owe less to one who gave you all at once the strength from which you can carry on for a long time than to one who daily confers something which on that day may be sufficient. Concerning these things, God gives daily what he may take away at any time. The free gift is not turned into something that is owed or earned [*debitum*] but the *modus donandi* is changed. Grace is not given according to merits—even the Pelagians forswear this—

54Ibid., 10:1411, E-F.

but should grace be abandoned, it would appear to have been given to those unworthy of it.[55]

Augustine had insisted that a person's natural choices were incapable of meriting grace. His understanding of the operation of grace at different levels of human deliberation and action, however, permitted Erasmus to involve natural virtues in a growth in grace with the confidence that he stood securely in an Augustinian, and therefore orthodox, tradition. Erasmus realized that Augustine in his own time ran the risk of playing into the hands of his Pelagian adversaries. Many of Augustine's descendants misread their master and they attributed too much independence to human will.[56] Luther's misreading, according to Erasmus, launched him in the opposite direction. Tempests of anathema were nevertheless unnecessary and they tended to distract Christians from what Erasmus conceived as a purely terminological problem. The war of words did not reflect an actual competition between grace and will, for such competition had no basis in the reality of the Christian life. Faithful to Colet and to the simple statement of divine and human coefficiency which lay behind and yet ever beyond the reach of subtle distinctions contrived to explain it, Erasmus returned in his *Hyperaspistes* to the place from which this study of salvation and reform proceeded and the place where he believed Augustine's true sentiments were to be found: "Let us consider Augustine, not yet a Christian."

Erasmus judged that Augustine's later polemics demonstrated considerable terminological sophistication. He found ("*reperit*") many names for grace, or, more precisely, for the work of grace. From these names,

---

[55]Ibid., 10:1531, F-1532, A: "Quanquam plausibilius est fateri in his non abesse Dei gratiam, hominis viriculas, per se invalidas, paulatim provehentis. Nihilo enim minus debeas ei, qui tibi semel fortem dedit, unde possis diu negotiari, quam qui quotidie conferat aliquid, quod in eum diem satis sit. Ad haec quotidie dat, cui semper in manu est quod dedit eripere. Non enim hic donum gratuitum vertitur in debitum, sed modus donandi mutatur. Nec hic gratia datur secundum merita, quod exsecrabantur etiam Pelagiani, sed vitatur, ne gratia dari videatur indignis."

[56]Ibid., 10:1480, E-F: "Quanto supercilio risit id quod citaram ex Propheta Zacharia, 'Convertimini ad me, & convertar ad vos,' cum ex hujusmodi locis Augustinus fateatur statui liberum arbitrium, in tantum ut periclitetur, ne is locus faciat pro Pelagio. Quibus ludibriis incessit verba imperandi?"

scholastics derived their elaborate distinctions; but, for Erasmus, it was far more significant that grace "found" Augustine struggling with his own faith and righteousness. The document that drew Erasmus's attention at this important point in his own argument's conclusion was none other than Augustine's *Confessions*.

> Let us consider Augustine, not yet a Christian, but at the crossroads contemplating that sect among all the others into which he might be initiated. He was then a Manichaean—not because he approved of Manichaeanism philosophically but lest he seem to be of no persuasion at all. He doubted concerning Christ, but he intended to subscribe to that which he came to know as the best.[57]

Erasmus recalled how Augustine listened attentively to Ambrose and to the counsel of other pious friends. Augustine shunned profane spectacles and games, and he read his Paul faithfully. He was generous with his alms and with his prayers. He kept only one concubine, and he treated her liberally. Erasmus considered it absurd to argue whether or not these earnest and morally upright acts merited grace. "We are terrified by the shadows of words." Preparation such as the one Augustine underwent was neither exclusively of grace nor exclusively of will.

> I have heard certain persons, whose sincere faith and life I have not known to be dishonest, saying: "If God would only give me a righteous will. . . ." I respond, yours is not capriciously to desire such a gift of God but also to solicit it. "In what way?" they inquire. Read the scriptures, I reply. Listen at worship, pray often, distribute money to the needy, trust your salvation to pious men, draw back as you are able from your sins. God's grace will not have been wanting in those things which stand out in your conduct. I judge that I have given pious counsel. Whoever desires that a good will be given to him does not altogether lack it. Whoever desires the gift of faith does not entirely lack faith, but what he has is imperfect and he wants divine help to perfect it. It is not of major moment whether one says that

---

[57]Ibid., 10:1531, B: "Proponamus Augustinum nondum Christianum, sed veluti in compito deliberantem, cui sectae potissimum esset initiandus. Nam Manichaeus erat, non quod eam probaret haeresim, sed ne nullius esse sectae videretur. De Christo dubitabat, aderat tamen hic animus, ut quam comperisset optimam, ei daret nomen."

these works were achieved by free choice or always by an assisting special grace raising us but not perfecting us.[58]

What matters, it seemed to Erasmus, is that the Christian does as Augustine did. If one only listens to Augustine, the profusion of words is as likely to confuse as to enlighten. Still, Erasmus, compelled to return to the issue raised by scholastics and by Luther, admitted the priority and necessity of grace for any upright and soteriologically significant human effort.

It is more plausible . . . that the little effort . . . is not without God's grace.[59]

---

[58]Ibid., 10:1531, D-E: "Verborum umbris territamur. . . . Sic enim audivi quosdam dicentes: Utinam Deus donaret mihi fidem: Utinam daret rectam voluntatem, quorum neque fidem sinceram & vitam improbam esse sciebam. Quibus respondebam: Tuum est non leviter optare tantum Dei donum, sed etiam ambire. Quibus inquiebant modis? Evolve, inquam, sacros Libros, adi sacras conciones, ora frequenter, eroga pecuniam in egenos, piis hominibus commenda salutem tuam, detrahe paulatim vitiis quod potes. Haec quae in te sita sunt praestanti, non defutura est Dei gratia: & arbitror me dedisse pium consilium. Qui optat sibi dari bonam voluntatem, non omnino caret ea: & qui optat fidei donum, non prorsus caret fide, sed quod habet imperfectum, optat auxilio divino perfici. Nec ita magni refert, utrum quis dicat haec opera exerceri per liberum arbitrium, an semper adspirante peculiari gratia, provehente non perficiente."

[59]Ibid., 10:1531, F. Also see Charles Trinkaus, "Erasmus, Augustine, and the Nominalists," *Archiv für Reformationsgeschichte* 67 (1976): 5-32. His point that Erasmus was a theologian of no mean accomplishment is well taken, but Trinkaus's comparison between the Augustinianism of the *Hyperaspistes* and the *facere quod in se est* principle of late medieval nominalism is somewhat overdrawn (pp. 21-22). Nominalists held various opinions about human ability to prepare for grace, and extremists believed that one could orient oneself advantageously without divine assistance and virtually compel divine favor and grace. See Karl Feckes, "Die Stellung der nominalistischen Schule zur aktuellen Gnade," *Römische Quartalschrift* 32 (1924): 157-65. As his use of Augustine's *Confessions* in the *Hyperaspistes* indicates, Erasmus was also concerned with advantages that might be gained from good behavior and sincere pursuit of God's grace. He was reasonably certain, however, that such behavior and pursuit was not independent of grace ("*Quanquam plausibilius est fateri in his non abesse Dei gratiam*"). Trinkaus reconstructs Erasmus's lengthy reference to the *Confessions*, but he stops short of this concluding and crucial remark. Erasmus's earlier notation of Augustine's good conduct prior to his confession of faith (*Enchiridion*, p. 92, lines 25-30) is more adaptable to the comparison intended by Trinkaus, but there Erasmus wished only to shame professed Christians with reports of the admirable virtues of unbelievers. It is fair to say that Erasmus addressed the problem of grace's relation to human will, convinced that the struggle that precedes the Christian's decisive restoration to God's favor and to righteousness was not without prevenient and persistent divine assistance.

Erasmus preferred the "applied theology" characteristic of his *Enchiridion*, but if forced to speculate about the origins and dynamics of the spiritual life, he was, with the help of Augustine, Colet, and, of course, St. Paul, equal to the task.

Conclusion

Erasmus was unable to satisfy his many friends and admirers who expected from him consistent leadership in the cause of church reform. A vast literature has accumulated atop the layer of disappointment that spread from Spain and Italy to Saxony in the early sixteenth century, but just when every possible explanation for Erasmus's various hesitancies and inconsistencies seems tried, a new and slightly different account is published. My point has not been, nor is it now, to offer an elaborate explanation for Erasmus's alleged failures but rather to understand, in part, the genealogy of Catholic reform and therefore to make somewhat more intelligible one of Erasmus's recognized successes. Still, from the perspective shaped in these pages, it is appropriate to urge clemency. Like Augustine, Erasmus owed to the confusions and conflicts of his own time his inability to press the implications of divine collaboration in personal histories and personal righteousness and steadfastly to apply those implications to the reform of his church. One could hardly be penetrating and persistent, not to mention persuasive, about the idea of collaboration when one lived constantly in the center of controversy. Too many challenges swirled around Erasmus. Obligations to defend himself and to clarify the limits of criticism crowded his editorial and interpretive work. His interest in the spiritual life and his commitment to Catholic reform never again combined as intimately and eloquently as they had in the *Enchiridion* of 1501 to illumine the relationship between personal behavior and institutional rehabilitation.

The connection between personal righteousness and institutional reform is familiar to students of the history of the Christian traditions. The Catholic reform tradition developed, in part, by osmosis, absorbing complaints about official misconduct and often making them privileged pronouncements. The reforming papacy's warfare against simony is perhaps the most dramatic example: its triumph is marked by Gratian's declaration, which bears an unmistakably Donatist imprint, that ordinations performed by simoniacal bishops are invalid.[1] Erasmus and, to a more limited extent, John Colet are parts of this tradition. Their legacy was not fully exploited at Trent, but the spirit of their campaigns filtered into the visitation protocols and proceedings that characterize the Counter-Reformation.[2] My interest in the Catholic reform, however, has taken me behind precedents and institutional consequences to the understanding of righteousness that associates humanistic Catholicism, and therefore Catholic reform, with a particular line of thought suggested by Augustine.

In the *Enchiridion* Erasmus was less parsimonious with his acknowledgments of debts owed to Augustine than Colet had been in his Oxford lectures. Were it not for his friendship with Colet, however, the influence of Augustine on Erasmus would have been different and, I suspect, more limited. Augustine proclaimed that sacrifice to God was not merely ceremonial but personal and moral and that "true and perfect sacrifice" transformed the self, as St. Paul suggested, into an instrument of God's

---

[1]*Concordia discordantium canonum*, 2, causa 1, q. 7, c. 24.

[2]In some circles the hunt for documents relating to visitation articles in this century bears striking resemblance to the hunt for fossils in the last. There exists a prevailing sense that archival discoveries are important links between Trent and the reform of church life, but prudence dictates the postponement of any judgment on the coherence of the continental Counter-Reformation until the materials from the visitation proceedings can be better orchestrated. Documents, however, have for years been profitably exploited in local histories, of which Karl Hengst's exhaustive evaluation of reforms in Paderborn is representative. See his *Kirchliche Reformen in Fürstbistum Paderborn unter Dietrich von Fürstenburg* 1585-1618 (Munich, 1974). Also see the collection of papers and the list of known "deposits" in Germany in *Die Visitation im Dienst der kirchlichen Reform*, Katholisches Leben und Kirchenreform in Zeitalter Glaubensspaltung 25/26 (Munster, 1967).

will and righteousness. Erasmus repeated this as a judgment on the church's excessive reliance on ritual and law, but his constructive intelligence, building upon his criticisms, identified Christianity with a moral universalism, echoing his Pauline and practical spirituality in the context of his modification of the cultural universalism of Italy's most ardent humanists. (Lorenzo Valla's famous axiom springs to mind: "*Ibi namque Romanum imperium est ubicumque Romana lingua dominatur.*") Like Rome, Christianity prospers in the lives and literature it inspires and not principally in the institutions and ceremonies that change, decay, and perish as does all else in the city of man. Erasmus would have admitted (in agreement with Augustine and Colet) that the inspired and righteous life was the spiritual sacrifice demanded by St. Paul and accomplished by all Christians who petition, accept, and collaborate with God's Spirit.[3]

This talk of sacrifice is not, of course, primarily about God, whose conjectural gain or enrichment from spiritual sacrifice was of little or no consequence for Augustine, Colet, and Erasmus. They grasped the moral rather than the speculative significance of spiritual sacrifice. This is also to say that, at their initiatives, Christianity was purposefully removed from disputes about divine foreknowledge, grace's irresistibility, and the sacraments' *ex opere operato* effectiveness—in short, from all aggregates of ideas that linked the Christian life to the intricacies of competing doctrines. Instead, Christianity was identified with the life of righteousness, with what might be called the "lived knowledge" of the mystery of divine collaboration in personal righteousness and, derivatively, in church reform. John Colet composed his lectures around the assertion that God's love makes the personality an instrument of righteousness and requires the Christian to make of life a sacrament, offering love to God and neighbor. Moreover, for Colet, the very experience of God's love and of the proximity of God's Spirit ("*Quia amamur . . .*") can only be "known" in the return of God's love (". . . *Deum redamus*") in faith, worship, and service. Of the three, service, I have argued, is the most important to Colet; and "lived knowledge" of God's presence in human

---

[3]See, for example, *De civ. Dei* 10.6.47; SAC, pp. 71-72, 79; and *Enchiridion*, p. 67, line 34-p. 68, line 14.

spirituality is indeed moral knowledge. As Erasmus would have it, the spiritual are identical with the ethical demands of life. These assertions about the redemptive possibilities and value of human action were what distinguished humanistic Catholicism from religious formalisms and from reigning speculative theologies of the late medieval period.

Long before Colet and Erasmus, Italian humanistic Catholics explicitly affirmed the significance of human intentionality and activity in the economy of salvation, and some Italians looked for guidance to Augustine. Petrarch's Augustine, in the first dialogue of the *Secretum*, repeats Ovid's admonition, "To wish for what you want is not enough; with ardent longing you must strive for it."[4] This faint remembrance of Augustine's own distinction between desire and longing, advanced also by Peter Lombard, is more characteristic of Italian Renaissance religion than its alleged anticlericalism; and it certifies that Augustine's more overtly polemical and anti-Pelagian writing had less to do with the confirmation of his impeccable credentials in humanist circles than his psalm commentaries and his own monumental psalm, the *Confessions*. It is noteworthy that Erasmus should seize the opportunity, at the conclusion of his *Hyperaspistes*, to rehearse Augustine's story of struggle and conversion. The *Confessions* is the capstone of Erasmus's treatise on grace, will, and righteousness, the treatise that happens to be his most thorough reply to incipient Lutheranism. But, notwithstanding his fascination with Italy, Erasmus belonged to northern Europe: his commentary on righteousness and reform in the *Hyperaspistes*, and therefore his recourse to Augustine's narrative, is rooted in the *Enchiridion*'s completion of John Colet's efforts to locate experiential as well as Pauline sources for theology. Certainly Augustine circulated widely through late medieval Europe; however, if I am correct, Colet's lectures and Erasmus's moral theology comprise an especially important chapter in the history of late medieval Augustinianism.

Colet's chief interest was the restoration of the Pauline doctrine of the Christian life. It is extremely difficult to determine to what extent he

---

4From Ovid's *Epistulae ex ponto* 3.1.35: "Velle parum est; cupias, ut re potiaris, oportet." The rather extravagant translation is William Draper's (*Petrarch's Secret* [London, 1891], p. 23).

formulated independent of Augustine his own "solutions," if they may be so dignified, to the problems of grace and will in human righteousness. The voluntarist mysticism of Augustine and Peter Lombard had been all but obscured by the dense forest of graces, habits, and partial merits that had grown around it since the thirteenth century. All that can reasonably be inferred is that Colet was eager to clear the "forest" in order to find St. Paul and to establish a closer relationship between doctrine and experience and that he stumbled across a favorite theme of Augustine's.

This inference has been, in part, anticipated, despite the scattered encomiastic remarks, emblematic of Erasmus's affection for and Victorian admiration of Colet, that have lured scholars from John Colet's genuine affinity with Augustine. Sears Jayne, most circumspect of the revisionists, wisely traded the notion that Colet's thinking was dominated by Neoplatonism for the realization that his dedication to St. Paul was fundamentally Augustinian. The meaning of this for Professor Jayne, however, is uncertain in places; and in one unfortunate summary it is reduced to Colet's general subscription to an "Augustinian ethics."[5] In fact, John Colet's likeness to Augustine is at once more recondite and more startling. His voluntarism and essential optimism were parts of a theology of grace that was more nuanced than the Augustinianisms of the Italian Renaissance though "under-stipulated" by comparison with scholastic adaptations of Augustinian soteriology. Colet resembles an Augustine more candidly theological than the one reclaimed in quattrocento Italian literature yet less sophisticated and unambiguous than the Augustine who can be pieced together from citations in late scholastic philosophy and theology. Indeed the very effort to trim the excesses from scholastic arguments may have revealed to Colet and then to Erasmus the structure of a basic but commonly ignored tension in Augustine's thought, a tension central to humanistic Catholicism.

Augustine insisted that God drew near to him and penetrated his heart without violence or injury. Although, at the conclusion of his autobiographical reflections in the *Confessions*, he was especially inspired by this intimacy, he also emphasized that humanity and divinity

---

[5]Jayne, *John Colet and Marsilio Ficino*, pp. 77-78.

were worlds apart.[6] Peter Lombard retained the tension in his recapitulation of Augustine's soteriology, but his presumption of an unmediated spiritual presence in personal righteousness profoundly demonstrated his sympathy with Augustine's sense of the mystery of divine intimacy and collaboration. Peter's unwillingness to specify further, to a considerable extent, occasioned developments that can be construed as reactions; the first to Peter and the second to the first. Later scholastics frequently assumed that intimacy and distance were conceptually bridged, with the greatest difficulty but nonetheless through the exertions of pious and well-schooled reason: hence the proliferation of categories, mediating habits and virtues, and graces. The Protestant reaction to this was shaped with unflinching hostility; and the tension in Augustine's thought, rather than being resolved, was apparently denied, as if the greatest of Latin theologians were as unsubtle as his scholastic interpreters were subtle.

The scholastic and Protestant reactions are powerful factors, as well they should be, in retelling the history of the Christian traditions and in recounting the fate of Augustine's ideas. They had, however, been instrumental in the virtual disappearance of "the man of Augustine," who, according to Peter Brown, "is always about to be engulfed in vast mysterious solidarities."[7] Later schoolmen seemed impatient with vast mysteries; the Protestants were intolerant of suggestions of solidarity and collaboration. Precisely for these reasons they find little place in a study of this sort. From the beginning I have been concerned with the mysterious solidarity that lay behind Augustine's acquired ability to will by all means and to persevere in righteousness, and behind Peter Lombard's identification of charity with divine presence. The same sense of mystery resurfaced in humanistic Catholicism's lean version of the schoolmen's efforts to bridge divine intimacy and distance, that is, in John Colet's description of righteousness as a living spiritual sacrament and in Erasmus's emphasis on the spirituality of the moral life. All this is characteristic of a mentality inclined to expect the miraculous in the moral and in the collaboration of divine and human wills in righteousness that allows one to speak of a voluntarist mysticism.

---

[6]*Conf.* 11.9.11.

[7]Peter Brown, *Augustine of Hippo* (Berkeley, 1969), p. 365.